# HOCKEY HALL OF FAME

# UNSTOPPABLE

Maurice Richard

# HOCKEY HALL OF FAME
## *UNSTOPPABLE*

### STEVE MILTON & MIKE RYAN

FIREFLY BOOKS

## A Firefly Book

Published by Firefly Books Ltd. 2016

First printing

Publisher Cataloging-in-Publication Data (U.S.)
A CIP record for this title is available from the Library of Congress

Library and Archives Canada Cataloguing in Publication
A CIP record for this title is available from Library and Archives Canada

Published in the United States by
Firefly Books (U.S.) Inc.
P.O. Box 1338, Ellicott Station
Buffalo, New York  14205

Published in Canada by
Firefly Books Ltd.
50 Staples Avenue, Unit 1
Richmond Hill, Ontario L4B 0A7

Printed in Canada

 We acknowledge the financial support of the Government of Canada.

### Photo Credits

**Hockey Hall of Fame**
Paul Bereswill 4-5, 25, 26, 27, 30, 38, 41, 43, 44, 46, 47, 48-49, 62, 63, 63, 70, 71, 74-75, 76, 77, 84-85, 107, 130, 131, 133, 138, 139; Studio Alain Brouillard 20; HHOF 10, 12 L&R, 14, 15, 22, 28-29, 34-35, 42, 51, 52. 57, 64, 65, 65, 68, 73, 75, 90, 112, 119, 120-121, 121, 123, 125, 128-129, 132-133; Fred Keenan 116-117; Doug MacLellan 61, 78-79, 79, 83, 86, 94, 98-99, 106, 134-135; Mecca 24, 66, 105, 124, 129; Frank Prazak 1, 6-7, 21, 22-23, 29, 37, 56, 65, 72-73, 80-81, 81, 110-111; Portnoy 32, 33, 36, 53, 67, 88, 89, 104, 118; Chris Relke 69, 96-97, 97, 102, 137, 140, 144, 145, 148; Dave Sandford 31, 35, 40, 58, 82, 83, 87, 95, 99,  100-101, 101, 103, 108-109, 109, 141, 146; Robert Shaver 122; Roger St. Jean/La Presse 115; Imperial Oil–Turofsky 8-9, 16-17, 18-19, 50-51, 91, 92, 93 113, 114

**Associated Press**
AP 126-127, 127; Al Behrman 143; Paul Chiasson 157; Mel Evans 155; Rusty Kennedy 141, 147; Denis Paquin 142; David J. Phillip 156; Gene J. Puskar 59; Kyodo News 153; Chris O'Meara 152-153; Pablo Martinez Monsivais 150, 151; Matt Slocum 154-155

**Cover**
Top: Doug MacLellan/HHOF
Bottom (L to R): O-Pee-Chee/HHOF, Justin Berl/Icon Sportswire, Mecca/HHOF, Graphic Artists/HHOF, Imperial Oil–Turofsky/HHOF

**Back Cover**
Top (L to R): HHOF, Paul Bereswill/HHOF
Bottom: Imperial Oil–Turofsky/HHOF

Wayne Gretzky

Phil Esposito

# TABLE OF CONTENTS

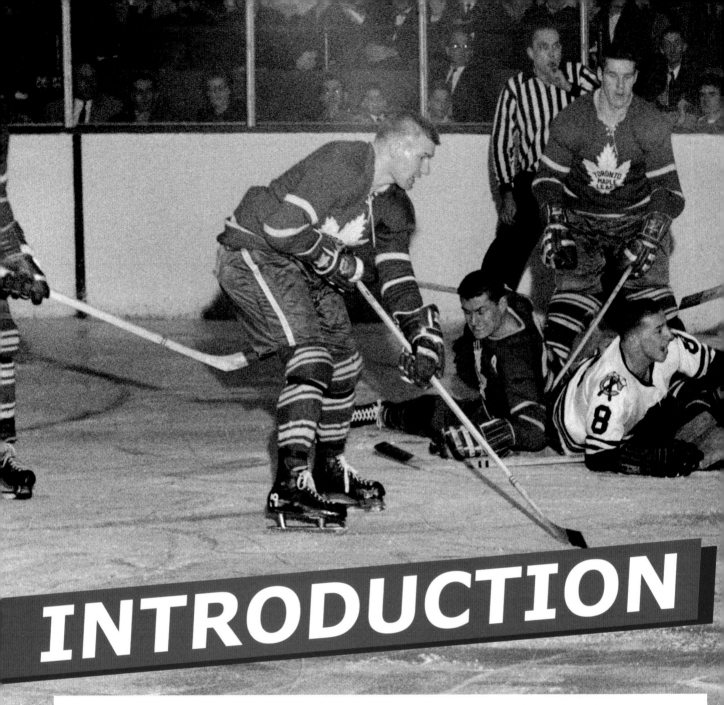

# INTRODUCTION

**F**IVE HUNDRED NHL regular-season goals. Let those words linger for a moment ...

*Five hundred*. That's a lot of rubber hitting twine.

Now consider this: at the conclusion of the 2015–16 season, only 43 NHLers had managed this stunning feat — less than 1 percent of anyone who's ever fired a puck in NHL history. Of those players, 32 have managed to find their way to the Hockey Hall of Fame.

"Exclusive" doesn't even begin to describe membership in the Hall's 500 Club.

The list is extraordinary, of course, and populated with legends like Maurice Richard, Gordie Howe, Wayne Gretzky and Mario Lemieux. But the stagger-ing level of achievement the members of this club attained becomes even more impressive considering those Hall of Famers who didn't manage — among all their feats — to score 500 goals.

Peter Stastny, who scored the second-most points (after Gretzky) in the decade of the 1980s, managed to score an incredible 450 career regular-season goals. His goal scoring and playmaking prowess is unquestioned, yet he's not in the club. Neither is the dynamic Darryl Sittler, who finished his career with the record for most points in a game and a total-goals mark of 484. Tantalizingly close, but not quite.

Those two players are among many extremely skilled marksmen who serve to illustrate just how

Bobby Hull

difficult hitting the 500-goal milestone is.

In a word, the players in this exclusive club were simply *unstoppable*.

Here for the first time, authors Steve Milton and Mike Ryan present the Hockey Hall of Fame's 500 Club. From Jean Béliveau to Steve Yzerman, Milton and Ryan share stories of game-winners, multi-goal games, scoring streaks and goals that changed the course of the league. These celebrated players were leaders, game breakers and record setters. They won championships — some guaranteed championships — and made their teammates better. They were the shining lights of the league and the most feared shooters in history.

Some goals, however, are undoubtedly bigger than others. Milton and Ryan take care to chronicle some of the most important goals ever scored in the chapter titled "Game-Breaking Goals." And hockey historian Eric Zweig provides his take on the early-era greats who, during a time when 500 goals was an unthinkable achievement, set the stage for the goal-scoring virtuosos who followed.

As Zweig contends in his essay, scoring was always the main point of the game. So please enjoy this celebration of those who did it often and did it best.

Steve Cameron,
Editor

# EARLY-ERA GOAL SCORERS

**Eric Zweig**

From the beginning, hockey has always been about scoring goals.

The Spalding *Ice Hockey and Ice Polo Guide* of 1898 may well be the earliest book written about the sport. Edited and compiled by J.A. Tuthill of the Montclair Athletic Club in Montclair, New Jersey, the book notes that the object of the game is simply "to drive the 'puck' between and through the opponent's goal posts."

One year later, future Hockey Hall of Famer Arthur Farrell wrote the first book on hockey published in Canada. He doesn't state them until chapter four, but Farrell's thoughts are exactly the same: "What is the objective point, the central idea, in the game of hockey? To score — to lift, slide, push or knock the puck through your opponent's goal."

Obviously, hockey's early-era stars played a different-looking game than the one we are familiar with today. With their equipment and training techniques, they couldn't skate like today's players or shoot like them either. It's just as hard to imagine early goaltenders lunging from post to post or sprawling to make saves — of course in the beginning, they couldn't, because the rules back then required them to remain on their feet at all times. Even as the rules loosened, acrobatic play was frowned upon. That was certainly an advantage for early-era scorers. Then again, the sticks they carried bore little resemblance to the rocket-launching composite sticks of today. And of course at the start, there was no forward passing.

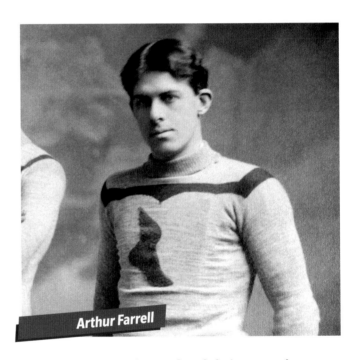
Arthur Farrell

Still, there were plenty of goals being scored — and the fans loved it.

## The 1890s and Early 1900s

This is Arthur Farrell's era. The game in those days was played with seven players on the ice, and yet teams from this time had very small rosters. Players were expected to play for a full 60 minutes. Substitutions were allowed only in the case of severe injury — and not always then. Being on the ice for the duration of the game certainly gave the top players more opportunities to score, as did the style of play. The need to pace themselves meant players tended to stick to their positions. Imagine the rink as a table hockey game, with slots that allow players to go only so far. Defensemen usually confined their activities to trying to stop goals in their own end. Forwards didn't do much back-checking. As a result, they got most of the goals, with the center — because he played in the middle — usually getting the most of all. The extra player (the seventh), known as the rover, was generally free to roam the ice, helping out on defense and on offense too. The rover was often a team's most talented player and so would also score a lot of goals. And everyone agreed that scoring goals, not preventing them, was the whole point.

In his book, Farrell turns to some of the greats of the game (circa 1899) to discuss how each position is properly played. The section on forwards is written by Farrell's teammate Harry Trihey, captain of the Montreal Shamrocks, who had just concluded their first of two consecutive seasons as Stanley Cup champions.

"The essentials of a forward," writes Trihey, "are science, speed, coolness, endurance and stickhandling, which embraces shooting … Science and speed are exercised at all times during the game; coolness is essential, especially when a forward is near his opponent's goal; endurance is taxed in the second half of the match, and stickhandling is a necessary quality whenever the player has the puck."

When it came specifically to scoring, Trihey believed, "most goals are scored on a rush, not from a scrimmage, and for this reason it is advisable not to lose too much energy in tussling for the puck behind the goal line." He also felt "it is a mistake to attempt to score when too far removed from the goal or at too great an angle to the side." His key piece of advice was that "the most successful shot for the goal is a lift that raises the puck only as high as the goal-minder's knee." Clearly, not all of Trihey's advice holds true anymore.

He is, however, one of hockey's first great scoring stars. Trihey made his debut at the highest level of the game, playing a single contest with the Shamrocks in the Amateur Hockey Association of Canada in 1896–97. A year later he played the full eight-game season and scored 3 goals. In 1898–99, Trihey broke out as hockey's best player, and the Shamrocks became the greatest team of the time. Trihey led the newly organized Canadian Amateur Hockey League (CAHL) with 19 goals in just seven games played that season. On February 4, 1899,

## Notable Early-Era Scorers

### DAN BAIN
Led the Manitoba and Northwest Hockey Association in scoring for five straight seasons with the Winnipeg Victorias, from 1894–95 through 1898–99, and became the first player in hockey history to score a Stanley Cup–winning goal in overtime, in 1901.

### TOMMY PHILLIPS
Led the Manitoba Hockey League in scoring for three straight seasons, from 1904–05 to 1906–07, and had all four goals in a 4–2 victory and three more in an 8–6 win as the Kenora Thistles swept the Montreal Wanderers to win the Stanley Cup in January 1907.

### ERNIE RUSSELL
Led the Eastern Canada Amateur Hockey Association with 42 goals in just nine games for the Montreal Wanderers in the 10-game 1906–07 season and added 12 goals in five Stanley Cup games, likely making him hockey's first 50-goal scorer at the game's highest level.

### MARTY WALSH
Ottawa Senators star led the Eastern Canada Hockey Association in scoring, with 42 goals in 12 games, in 1908–09. He also led the National Hockey Association in scoring, with either 35 or 37 goals in 16 games, in 1910–11 and added 10 goals in a Stanley Cup game against Port Arthur on March 16, 1911.

### DIDIER PITRE
Known as Cannonball for his powerful shot, he played hockey at the highest level from 1903–04 through 1922–23. Pitre led the International Hockey League with 41 goals in 22 games in 1905–06 and had 30 goals in 20 games for the Montreal Canadiens in the National Hockey Association in 1914–15.

### CYCLONE TAYLOR
A high-scoring defenseman with the Ottawa Senators and Renfrew Millionaires in the east, he moved west and led the Pacific Coast Hockey Association in goals three times and points five times with the Vancouver Millionaires between 1912 and 1919, while playing as a center and rover.

he scored 10 goals in the Shamrocks' 13–4 victory over Quebec. No other player in hockey history has ever scored more goals in a regular season game in a league that competed for the Stanley Cup.

A year later Trihey led the CAHL in scoring again, and the Shamrocks repeated as Stanley Cup champions. In six Stanley Cup challenge games over those two seasons, Trihey had 15 goals. Even so, his biggest contributions to hockey can't be counted among his statistics. Trihey and his linemates (Farrell and another future Hall of Famer, Fred Scanlan) are said to have introduced new strategies to the game by passing the puck among themselves rather than relying on individual rushes. This so-called scientific approach or combination game was a revelation — even though at the time the Shamrocks could make only drop passes and cross-ice maneuvers, as forward passing hadn't yet been introduced. Before his final season as a player in 1900–01, Trihey also served on the committee that recommended the CAHL adopt goal nets rather than continue to use posts with no mesh, as was the tradition at the time.

The CAHL also gave rise to scoring stars Russell "Dubbie" Bowie and Frank McGee. Bowie topped the CAHL in goals in four of five seasons from 1900–01 through 1904–05 and added another goal-scoring crown in the Eastern Canada Amateur Hockey Association in 1907–08. All told, Bowie scored 239 goals in just 80 games played with the Montreal Victorias in his 10 seasons at hockey's highest level. That's an average of nearly 3 goals per game! Many fans from his generation considered Bowie to be the greatest player they ever saw, and yet (perhaps because he won only one Stanley Cup series, in his rookie season of 1898–99) he is mostly forgotten today. But not every name from this early era is beyond recognition.

Like Bowie, Frank McGee averaged 3 goals per game in his career, although he played just four seasons at hockey's highest level. From 1902–03 through 1905–06, McGee played only 23 regular-season games but scored at least 68 goals (some sources say 71). In addition, his Ottawa Hockey Club — commonly referred to as the Silver Seven — held the Stanley Cup for nearly all of those four seasons, allowing McGee to take part in 22 playoff games, in which he recorded more than 60 goals (63 or 64 depending on the source). Fourteen of McGee's goals came in a single game on January 16, 1905, when he led Ottawa to a 23–2 victory over Dawson City in a Stanley Cup challenge. His exploits are all the more amazing considering he'd suffered a severe loss of vision after taking a puck in the face during a game

Harry Trihey

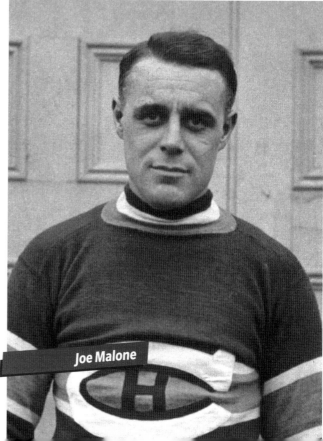

Joe Malone

in 1900. One hundred years after losing his life in 1916 as a soldier in World War I, "One-Eyed Frank McGee" remains a hockey legend.

## The NHL's First Scoring Star

Many fans have heard of Joe Malone. He's the player whose single-season NHL goal-scoring record was surpassed by Maurice "Rocket" Richard when the Rocket potted 50 goals in 50 games in 1944–45. Malone's record — 44 goals in just 20 games played with the Montreal Canadiens in 1917–18 — propelled him to mythical status, but Malone's reputation as a scorer was already well established.

Many early-era rules had already changed when Malone tore up the NHL in its debut season. The National Hockey Association (NHA, forerunner of the NHL) moved to three 20-minute periods instead of two 30-minute halves for its second season in 1910–11, and then dropped the rover in 1911–12. The rival Pacific Coast Hockey Association introduced forward passing in 1913–14 and allowed goalies to drop to the ice beginning in 1916–17. The NHL didn't follow through on that rule until midway through its inaugural season of 1917–18, and didn't introduce forward passing until 1918–19.

Malone's 44-goal season meant he scored at a clip of 2.20 goals per game, giving him the oldest unequaled mark in the *NHL Official Guide & Record Book* — and it's one that's not likely to be broken. The feat, however, was nothing out of the ordinary for the player known as Phantom Joe. Five years before the formation of the NHL, Malone led the NHA with 43 goals in 20 games for the Quebec Bulldogs in 1912–13. In that league's final season of 1916–17, he topped the circuit again, although Malone's 41 goals in 19 games actually tied him with Frank Nighbor of the Ottawa Senators. Returning to Quebec from Montreal in 1919–20, Malone led the NHL with 39 goals in 24 games, including 7 against the Toronto St. Pats on January 31, 1920, and 6 against the Ottawa Senators on March 10. The seven-goal game is another of Malone's solo records that may never be broken, and yet he'd had better nights on two occasions earlier in his career. Malone scored nine times in a Stanley Cup game for Quebec on March 8, 1913, and had 8 goals against the Montreal Wanderers in the NHA on February 28, 1917.

In all, Malone scored a league-record 179 goals in

123 games in the NHA, 143 goals in 126 NHL games, and another 23 goals in leagues that predated both, giving him a total of 345 goals for his career (which, depending on sources, was either 276 or 280 regular-season games).

## Montreal's Other Game Breaker

Joe Malone shared the ice with another goal-scoring maestro in the fierce Newsy Lalonde — the two were teammates for the NHL's first two seasons.

Suiting up in no fewer than nine leagues that were eligible (or attempted to challenge) for the Stanley Cup in the 23 years from 1904 to 1927, Lalonde played in 341 pro-league games and scored an amazing 449 goals. He won scoring titles (either goals or points or both) in the Ontario Professional Hockey League, the NHA (twice), the Pacific Coast Hockey Association, the NHL (twice) and the Western Canada Hockey League. He played for literally a dozen teams in his career, but Lalonde is most closely associated with the Montreal Canadiens, for whom he scored the first goal in franchise history on January 5, 1910. He remained with Montreal for all but one season through 1921–22.

Lalonde came from Cornwall, Ontario, and it's debatable how much French he actually spoke, but it was his speed and skill — along with teammates Jack Laviolette and Didier Pitre — that earned the Canadiens their Flying Frenchmen moniker back in the NHA.

In the words of Charles Coleman, whose three-volume set *The Trail of the Stanley Cup* in the 1960s was the first great work on early hockey, Lalonde was not just a great scorer but "a great fighter with a fiery temper [who] went after opponents, spectators and even teammates on occasion … A born leader, he was almost always the captain or playing manager of his team. There were no desultory performances without incurring the whiplash of his tongue."

As would Maurice Richard a generation later, Lalonde drew a crowd. Coleman writes, "His followers turned out to cheer him, and others bought their way in to scream, 'Get Lalonde.'"

Newsy scored 9 goals in a game for the Renfrew Millionaires of the NHA on March 11, 1910, and had 8 for Toronto in the Ontario pro league on February 29, 1908. His three career six-goal games include the first one in NHL history on January 10, 1920. His

Howie Morenz

mark of 5 goals in an NHL playoff game in Montreal's 6–3 win over Ottawa on March 1, 1919, has been tied by Maurice Richard, Darryl Sittler, Reggie Leach and Mario Lemieux but is yet to be broken.

## The Torch Is Passed

Montreal's line of scoring stars was continued when Howie Morenz, the "Stratford Streak," joined the Canadiens in 1923–24, two seasons after Lalonde traveled west to play in the Western pro leagues.

It was around this time that changes were coming for the NHL. When the league first introduced forward passing in 1918–19, it was allowed only in the neutral zone. As the league grew — from a low of three teams playing just 18 games that year to ten teams playing 44 games in 1926–27 — rosters began to expand as well. Some star players (mostly defensemen, but a few forwards) were still playing close to 60 minutes a night, but many teams now rotated two forward lines. By the end of the decade, some clubs utilized three. Bigger rosters and better-rested players meant stronger defensive hockey, and offense began to decline. In 1928–29, Toronto's Ace Bailey led the NHL with just 22 goals in 44 games, while George Hainsworth of the Canadiens

Nels Stewart

posted 22 shutouts and a 0.92 goals-against average. The NHL finally permitted forward passing everywhere on the ice the following season, and scoring predictably skyrocketed.

No one had scored 40 goals since Joe Malone's 44 in 1917–18. But in 1929–30, Boston's Cooney Weiland (43 goals), his teammate Dit Clapper (41 goals) and Montreal's Morenz (40 goals) hit the mark. All three were future members of the Hockey Hall of Fame, but only Morenz enjoys the mythic status of Frank McGee, Joe Malone and Newsy Lalonde.

Morenz initially had cold feet about the NHL. He signed his first contract during the summer of 1923, but under pressure to stay at home and continue his amateur career, he fretted about becoming a professional and losing his amateur status if he failed to make a good impression in the NHL.

He needn't have worried.

Known as the Stratford Streak for his skating skill (as well as the hometown in Ontario he'd been afraid to leave behind), Morenz combined blazing speed and tremendous agility to become the NHL's biggest offensive star. Playing center alongside left-winger Aurèle Joliat (who would be his linemate for most of his career), the rookie Morenz helped

the Canadiens win the Stanley Cup in 1924. They won it again in 1930 and 1931. Morenz led the league in goals and points in 1927–28 and won a second scoring title in 1930–31, while also winning the Hart Trophy as MVP in both seasons. The following season he became the first player to win the Hart three times.

Though Morenz came from English Ontario, he was the darling of Montreal and the very epitome of the Flying Frenchmen. On March 17, 1932, Morenz picked up his 334th career point to become the NHL's all-time leader in points. His 249th career goal on December 23, 1933, made him the leading goal-scorer as well. However, injuries were beginning to slow him down, and after the 1933–34 season, Morenz was dealt to Chicago. He split the 1935–36 season between the Black Hawks and the New York Rangers but returned to Montreal the following year. Tragically, his career ended when he suffered a badly broken leg during a game on January 28, 1937. He died a few weeks later, on March 8, of a pulmonary embolism while still in hospital. Morenz's funeral was held on March 11, 1937, at center ice in the Montreal Forum. About twelve thousand people attended. Almost as many stood outside the building to pay tribute. Thousands more lined the streets en route to the cemetery in order to pay their last respects.

Morenz had scored 271 goals in his career, but during his final season of 1936–37, his NHL record was surpassed by Nels Stewart. Stewart had been born in Montreal but was raised in Toronto. He later played hockey in Cleveland for five seasons between 1920 and 1925, leading the U.S. Amateur Hockey Association in goals four times. He returned to the city of his birth to play for the Montreal Maroons as an NHL rookie in 1925–26. Stewart led the league with 34 goals and 42 points during the 36-game season, earning the Hart Trophy as MVP and leading the Maroons to a Stanley Cup championship in just their second season in the league.

Stewart was nowhere near the speedy skater that Howie Morenz was, but the deadly accuracy of his shot earned him the nickname Old Poison. He played in the NHL until 1939–40, scoring a career-best 39 goals in the high-scoring season of 1929–30 and leading the league for a second time with 23 goals in 1936–37. In his 16 NHL seasons, Stewart finished among the top 10 in goals 13 times and ended his career with 324. He remained the league's career goal-scoring leader until being surpassed by Maurice Richard on November 8, 1952.

\*      \*      \*

Maurice Richard had many admirers, but none so credible as the great Newsy Lalonde. The former Montreal goal-scorer remained a lifelong Canadiens fan. When he got his first look in 1942 at the man who would one day pass him as hockey's goal-scoring champion, he could see the greatness in the player who would be called Rocket.

"He's the best rookie to show in a long time," Lalonde told Dink Carroll of the *Montreal Gazette* about Richard. "He's got hockey instinct and does everything right. Even when he falls down, he looks good … The boy's a natural. [His] timing is perfect."

Harry Trihey — who died in December 1942 — hadn't said anything about timing to Art Farrell in 1899. If he'd ever seen the Rocket in action, he might have.

Richard's timing, though, wasn't limited to his relentless pursuit of goals; he had timing in a theatrical sense too. His 325th NHL goal, the one that broke Nels Stewart's career NHL record, came exactly ten years to the day that Richard had scored his first NHL goal. From then on, every goal Richard scored set a new NHL record. His 400th came on December 18, 1954, against Chicago's Al Rollins — the same man he had beaten for goal number 325.

Entering the 1957–58 season, Richard was the oldest man in the NHL. By then he'd scored 493 career goals (sailing well past Lalonde's career professional goal tally of 449), and he notched 6 more in Montreal's first five games to reach 499. His 500th goal — again against Chicago — on October 19, 1957, set off a huge celebration at the Montreal Forum.

Though he'd play until 1960 and help Montreal win the Stanley Cup three more times, Maurice Richard's 500th goal was the last great moment of his career. Wayne Gretzky has pushed the NHL record to 894 goals, but the milestone Richard reached nearly 60 years ago — like his 50 goals in a single season — remains the benchmark against which all great scorers are measured.

Maurice Richard holds his 324th goal puck, tying him with Nels Stewart for most career NHL goals.

Jean Béliveau

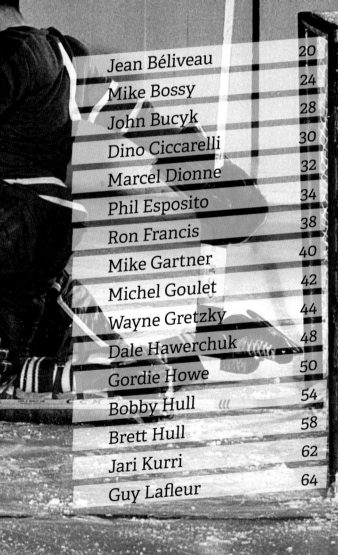

# 500 CLUB

# JEAN BÉLIVEAU

## 3 Goals in 44 Seconds

Legend has it that the Montreal Canadiens were so enamored with Jean Béliveau that they bought the entire Quebec Senior Hockey League (QSHL) to get him into the team's famed *sainte-flanelle*.

Béliveau was playing for the Quebec Aces, and he was fiercely loyal to his team. And although the QSHL was officially an amateur league, between playing hockey and doing promotional work for local businesses, Béliveau was earning more than anyone in the NHL. But in May of 1953, the Quebec league voted to turn pro. The question of Montreal's purchasing the league is the debate of hockey scholars, as is the Canadiens' influence on the QSHL's vote; however, what isn't disputed is that Montreal owned Béliveau's professional rights. Playing for the Aces was no longer an option, and in October he signed a five-year contract with Montreal. Béliveau's arrival altered the course of the franchise, and three years later it would change the rules of the NHL.

The elegant Béliveau, who scored his first NHL hat trick in 1952 while on a three-game tryout, was a contrast and complement to the fury and fire of Canadiens star Maurice "Rocket" Richard.

"He is a perfect coach's hockey player because he studies and learns," said Canadiens general manager Frank Selke of Béliveau. "He's moving and planning all the time, thinking out the play required for each situation. A perfectionist."

That meticulousness explains why Béliveau wasn't happy in November 1955, even though the Canadiens were in first place and he had 14 points in the team's first 12 games.

"I don't think I was ever so discouraged as I was at the start of the 1955–56 season," said Béliveau in Andy O'Brien's book *Fire-Wagon Hockey*. "I must have hit fifteen goalposts before Toe Blake told me to start shooting at the net, rather than at a particular spot, until I broke my slump. Sure enough, a couple did, and I did all right."

Playing the Boston Bruins on a Saturday night at the Montreal Forum, Béliveau was more than all right. His second career hat trick was historic and game changing.

The Bruins were up 2–0 on goals by Leo Boivin and Doug Mohns when Boston's Cal Gardner was

Jean Béliveau receives the Hart Trophy from Gordie Howe, 1964.

penalized with 10 seconds left in the first period. Just 16 seconds into the second period, Hal Laycoe joined Gardner in the penalty box to put the Canadiens up two men.

First-year coach Blake wisely sent out defensemen Doug Harvey and Tom Johnson with his all-world forward line of Béliveau, Richard and Bert Olmstead.

At 42 seconds of the second period, Béliveau redirected a pass from Olmstead behind goalie Terry Sawchuk to make it 2–1. Just 26 seconds later the two combined for Béliveau's 2nd to tie the game, and moments after that he had his 3rd goal of the power play, and the Habs had a 3–2 lead.

At 44 seconds it was the fastest hat trick in Canadiens history and second fastest in NHL history, after the Chicago Black Hawks' Bill Mosienko, who scored 3 in 21 seconds in 1952.

Olmstead had 3 assists on the power play and added another as Béliveau scored his 4th goal of the night — at even strength — in the third period as Montreal went on to win, 4–2. It was the first of Béliveau's three career four-goal games.

Playing the Bruins again a day later, Béliveau scored a 5th goal in a 3–3 tie. The weekend tear put him on top of the league with 19 points.

By season's end, Béliveau had 47 goals and 88 points in 70 games to win the Art Ross and Hart Trophies. He added 12 goals in 10 playoff games as Montreal lifted the first of five straight Stanley Cups in 1956.

Less heralded were Béliveau's 143 penalty minutes in 1955–56, good for third in the NHL. Though he was known to play with class and respect, when opponents took liberties with the 6-foot-3, 205-pound

superstar, he knew how to take care of himself and earn his space.

"He had size, strength, reach. He could really shoot the puck, and he was tougher than you might remember. If you got close to him, you got a cross-check," recalled teammate Dick Duff after Béliveau died in 2014. "It was a treat to play with him, a treat to watch him play. And he had time for everybody. No matter who it was. No matter what the situation was.

"He was a statesman for us. If there was someone to meet, he met them. If the prime minister came into our room, it was Jean who spoke to him. He could handle any situation. He could have been governor general and turned that down. I think he would have been perfect for that job."

On February 11, 1971, at the Forum, 39-year-old Béliveau had the 18th and last hat trick of his career, also becoming the fourth player in NHL history to reach 500 goals, after Richard, Gordie Howe and Bobby Hull.

His milestone goal was scored against rookie goaltender Gilles Gilbert of the Minnesota North Stars. After the game he sought out Gilbert, who was standing with his parents in the Forum concourse.

"He came up to me and, almost apologetically, told

me that, it didn't matter who would have been in net tonight, it was a night where everything went his way," remembered Gilbert. "He told me that I would have a long and successful career in the NHL, gave me his hand and left. It's special. I don't think anybody else would have done that."

At the end of the 1970–71 season, Béliveau had 507 career goals, and he capped his final season with the 10th Stanley Cup of his career and fifth as captain of the Canadiens. After receiving the Cup in Chicago, he lifted it over his head and took it for a victory lap, knowing it was his last as a player. That sort of celebration is now a tradition.

"I am not merely celebrating the Canadiens' triumph," said Béliveau of his trip around the ice. "I am celebrating the superb game of ice hockey and what it means to all of us."

Béliveau was part of seven more titles as a member of the Canadiens' front office. His name is engraved on the Cup a record 17 times.

Béliveau also had a lasting impact on the NHL rulebook. Back in 1955–56, the Canadiens scored multiple goals on a single power play eight times, including Béliveau's 44-second power-play hat trick on November 5.

In January 1956 at the urging of rival general managers, NHL president Clarence Campbell discussed allowing penalized players to return to the ice after a power-play goal instead of serving the entire two minutes regardless of how many goals were scored. At the 39th annual board of governors meeting in June, he officially introduced Rule 26(c), known colloquially as "the Canadiens Rule." It stated: "If while a team is 'shorthanded' by one or more minor or bench minor penalties, the opposing team scores a goal, the first of such penalties shall automatically terminate."

The six teams voted 5–1 in favor of the rule change. The lone dissenting vote came from Montreal. When it was suggested to NHL GMs that the Montreal power play was the impetus for the change, Boston's Lynn Patrick responded, "That's nonsense."

Montreal's Selke, though, wasn't so sure. "You might outvote me on that one. But you'll never convince me of its justice. In all the years of Detroit's dominance and their almighty power play, there was no suggestion of such a change. Now Canadiens have finally built one, and you want to introduce a rule to weaken it …

"Go get a power play of your own."

# MIKE BOSSY

## 50 Goals in 50 Games

"**I** told the Canadiens to draft him in 1977, but they wouldn't listen to me," said Montreal legend Maurice Richard of Mike Bossy, the wiry local star with the quick release.

"They said he wasn't good enough defensively. What the Canadiens didn't understand is when you can score goals like he can, you don't watch your man. He watches you."

Bossy grew up in Ahuntsic, a borough of Montreal, where Richard spent much of his life. The kid who once scored 23 goals in a game and 170 in a season joined the major junior Laval National at 14. After 309 goals in four junior seasons, Bossy was still passed over by 12 teams, including the New York Rangers and the Toronto Maple Leafs twice each.

The New York Islanders picked Bossy 15th overall, and in his first training camp, coach Al Arbour put him on a line with Bryan Trottier and Clark Gillies. The trio would become one of the most potent and productive in NHL history.

In 1977–78, Bossy proved Richard's prescience: he became one of 23 players in NHL history to score 50 goals in a season, as he set a rookie record with 53 and was named rookie of the year.

After scoring more than 50 in each of the next two seasons, including a career-high 69 in 1978–79, Bossy quietly set a goal for himself in 1980–81: to score 50 goals in 50 games. Only Richard had done that, 36 years earlier in 1944–45.

Bossy had 25 goals in his first 23 games, but it wasn't until after he scored his 36th goal — with six hat tricks to that point — and the normally reticent Bossy admitted to a reporter that he wanted to break Phil Esposito's record of 76 goals, that it became a story.

Other teams also took note and did their best to prevent Bossy from matching the Rocket's milestone against them. He still managed 48 goals through 47 games, and in Game 48 the Calgary Flames were focused more on thwarting Bossy than winning.

"I was very disappointed in the way Calgary played," said Islanders captain Denis Potvin. "All they did was check. They were down, 2–0, and they didn't seem the least bit interested in playing offensively. All they wanted to do, it seemed, was protect their net and stop Bossy from scoring."

Mike Bossy with his 50-goal puck on January 24, 1981.

Bossy was also held goal-less in Game 49 against the Detroit Red Wings, despite some gilt-edged chances, but at least the defending Stanley Cup–champion Islanders were winning.

"I should have given Bossy my glasses," said Arbour. "Two chances at an empty net. But if they won't go in, they won't go in. You know Bossy. He can still explode at any time. I can't complain, though, with back-to-back shutouts."

Bossy wasn't the only one chasing history. Charlie Simmer of the Los Angeles Kings was also on a torrid goal-scoring pace. He had 46 goals in 49 games, and in his 50th, a matinee on January 24, 1981, he had 3 goals, leaving him one shy of Richard's achievement.

A few hours after the Kings game, Bossy and the Islanders were playing at home against the Quebec Nordiques in their 50th game of the season. He was

still sitting on 48 goals, and when he was held without a shot after two periods, it looked as though he'd join Simmer in coming tantalizingly close.

Bossy spent the second intermission in a bathroom stall, smoking cigarettes and pondering what he'd say to the media after the game.

But with just over five minutes left and the game tied, 4–4, Bossy scored his 49th on a backhand, and at 18:31 he took a cross-ice pass from Trottier at the left faceoff circle and scored his 50th on goalie Ron Grahame.

"It was not an easy journey," remembered Bossy years later. "I began our 48th game with 48 goals. No goals in two straight games left me with having to score two in Game 50. I cut it even closer by waiting until the last two minutes, precisely 1:29, to score No. 50. I was dancing on the ice, there was bedlam

in the crowd and one of my personal hockey career objectives was accomplished."

His memorable and exuberant goal jig was an expression of pure joy and relief.

"The hardest part was never being able to be satisfied with what I had accomplished in any one game. I always had another game to go on to. There were times when I had a couple of three-goal games, but I didn't have time to savor them because you had to go out the next night and stay on pace. It was a constant whirlwind."

According to broadcaster Dick Irvin: "It was a great television shot of him doing a tap dance after that goal. He told me once he was embarrassed by it now, the way he celebrated."

When Bossy got back to the dressing room after the 7–4 win, he got a phone call from Richard, congratulating him on matching his accomplishment.

Richard, who received a letter from Joe Malone when he broke his record of 44 goals set in 1917–18, also sent Bossy a telegram that read in part: "I knew one day my record would be surpassed or tied, but I had always hoped that it would be by the player from Ahuntsic that I have admired from the start. We are proud of you here in Quebec."

Bossy went on to score 68 goals, and he had another 17 and a record 35 points in 18 playoff games to lead the Islanders to their second straight Stanley Cup.

Only one season after Bossy's 50 in 50, Wayne Gretzky scored 50 goals in 39 games. The Great One managed to pot 50 goals in fewer than 50 games

Mike Bossy scores his 50th goal (left) and celebrates with teammates on January 24, 1981.

twice more, and since then only Mario Lemieux and Brett Hull have done it.

Bossy is tied with Gretzky for a record nine seasons with more than 50 goals, and only Bossy did it in consecutive seasons. The only year when he didn't hit the 50-goal plateau was 1986–87, his 10th and final season, when back problems limited him to 63 games.

Bossy retired in 1987 at the age of just 30, with five seasons of 60 or more goals, four Stanley Cups, three Lady Byng Trophies and countless goals left in his hands.

In a career cut short by injury, Bossy might have been the purest goal-scorer in NHL history. With 573 goals in 752 regular-season games, he's the all-time leader in goals per game, at 0.762. That puts him ahead of Cy Denneny and Babe Dye in the early

20th century, and Gretzky, Lemieux and Hull in the modern era.

Bossy was inducted into the Hall of Fame in 1991, and 24 years later he was reunited with the puck that he used to score his 50th goal in 50 games. His daughter had actually given it to her swim coach as a thank-you gift, and after Bossy refused to take it back, it was sold on eBay.

Gavin Maloof, who owns the Palms hotel in Las Vegas and is a minority owner of the city's forthcoming NHL franchise, bought the puck and gave it back to Bossy.

"We need to get this puck," he said. "It means a lot to Mr. Bossy. Fifty goals in 50 games. Only a handful of people have ever done that. I needed to buy this puck. I don't care how much it costs."

# JOHNNY BUCYK

## Clearing the Runway for Orr to Take Flight

I t's one of the most enduring images in hockey history: Bobby Orr, the man who altered the course of the Boston Bruins and the game of hockey itself, flying through the air after being tripped by St. Louis Blues defenseman Noel Picard. Just moments before he took flight, Orr had scored the overtime goal that gave the Bruins their first Stanley Cup championship in 29 years.

But the game had gone into overtime only because the vastly underrated Johnny Bucyk tipped in John McKenzie's shot at 13:28 of the third period to tie the score at 3.

When Orr arrived in the fall of 1966, the Bruins' prospects changed immediately, although they would finish last in his rookie season. For Bucyk, 1966–67 was the eighth straight season in which he'd missed the playoffs with the Bruins. For many of those years, the large left-winger with the reputation for clean play was one of the only reasons to watch the moribund Bruins.

It was a symbol of continuity and hard work that the second-most important Bruins goal in four decades would come from the man who had been the heart of the franchise for 13 years. Bucyk had set

up his more famous teammates for goals and scored more than anyone cared to notice, all while playing third fiddle among NHL left-wingers to Bobby Hull and Frank Mahovlich.

He had been to the Stanley Cup Final only twice before; the most recent was a six-game loss to the dynastic Montreal Canadiens in the spring of 1958, his first year in Boston.

"I had waited a dozen years for that moment, and I was going to enjoy it," Bucyk recalled of hoisting the Stanley Cup for the first time. The Bruins didn't have an official captain in 1969–70, but Bucyk's teammates made sure he was the one to lift the Cup before anyone else, because of what he'd meant to the franchise and the horrible years he'd endured with class and humility before the Bruins finally reached the top.

Bucyk had been captain in Orr's rookie season, succeeding Leo Boivin, but he and coach Harry Sinden thought it might be better to spread the leadership chores around. So for six years he shared the duties with the likes of Phil Esposito, Ted Green and Ed Westfall.

"We worked together, and whatever had to be done, we did it," he explained.

When Sinden became GM, he reinstated Bucyk as captain for four more seasons, and since his retirement as a player in 1978, Bucyk has worked in a number of roles for the Bruins. With the exception of Milt Schmidt, no Bruin has been as closely tied to the franchise for as long as Bucyk.

Fittingly, Schmidt, whose playing career in Boston stretched from 1937 to 1955, was Bucyk's coach for seven years in Boston. And on December 2, 1967, when Bucyk scored his 229th and 230th goals as a Bruin, it was Schmidt's team record that he broke. Schmidt, by now the club's rookie GM, was in attendance. To illustrate how quickly the team's fortunes were changing, that game was the Bruins' 10th home win of the season, equaling their total for all of 1966–67.

Bucyk was almost always overshadowed: by Red Wings stars when he began his career in Detroit; by Terry Sawchuk, for whom he was traded; by Vic Stasiuk and Bronco Horvath, his one-time teammates on the Uke line; and by Phil Esposito, Bobby Orr and Gerry Cheevers when the Bruins finally caught and surpassed the Canadiens. Bucyk nevertheless put up Hall of Fame numbers, and when he retired, he was the highest-scoring left-winger of all time and the fourth leading scorer in NHL history. He was the left wing on the Bruins' prolific power play — one of the best in history — firing and redirecting shots from his office about four feet in front of the crease.

Until Orr made hockey — and photographic — history, Bucyk was among the favorites for the Conn Smythe Trophy as most valuable performer of the 1970 playoffs. He scored a hat trick in Game 1, including the first goal of the final, and the penultimate goal of the series gave him at least one in each game of the sweep.

"I've thought of myself as a spear carrier, not a star," he has said. "It has added up. I'm not a glamor guy and I've just gone along, getting what I could out of every game."

And he never got more out of any game than the one he sent into overtime for Bobby Orr to immortalize.

29

# DINO CICCARELLI

## From Undrafted to Rookie Record Setter

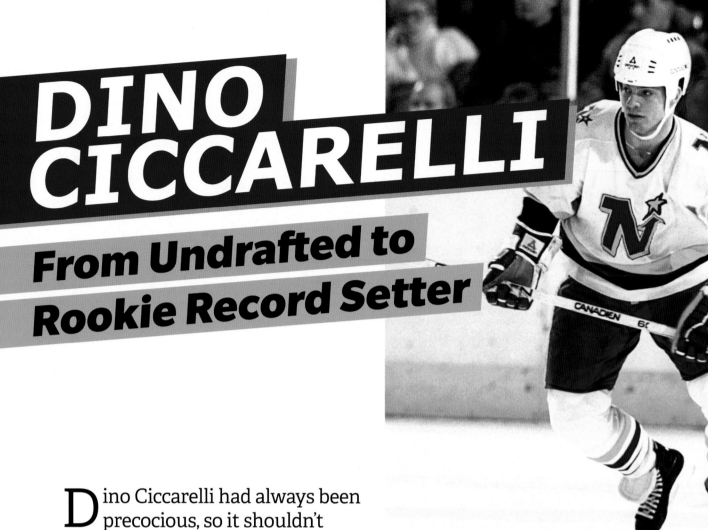

Dino Ciccarelli had always been precocious, so it shouldn't have come as a surprise when he became an NHL playoff prodigy at the tender age of 21.

When Ciccarelli was 15, he played for his hometown Sarnia Legionnaires with 20-year-olds, after the coach convinced his father he wouldn't get killed. Vic Ciccarelli, who immigrated to Canada from Italy in the 1950s, may not have played hockey, but he was his son's inspiration on the ice.

"I think it's why I was never satisfied as a hockey player and always pushed for more," says Dino. "I didn't care how big opponents were or how much it hurt; I wanted to stick my nose in there. Dad did anything to make money, to support his family. He's been my biggest fan … He drove me pretty hard. He's meant everything."

Ciccarelli joined the major junior London Knights at 16, and in his first season he had 82 points in 66 games and 24 points in 20 postseason matches. The following year he led the league in goals, with 72, but because of his relatively small stature (5-foot-10), he went undrafted. After another year of being passed over in the draft, the Minnesota North Stars wisely

signed him as a free agent in 1979.

Called up from the North Stars minor-league affiliate in Oklahoma for the final 32 games of the 1980–81 regular season, Ciccarelli made a splash when he averaged almost a point per game leading up to the 1981 playoffs. But the unheralded right-winger was just warming up.

In the first round — a sweep of the Boston Bruins — Ciccarelli had 6 points, including a goal and 3 assists in a 9–6 Game 2 victory. Facing the Buffalo Sabres in round two, he had another 6 points, four of them goals. And in the Stanley Cup semifinal against the Calgary Flames, he had a hat trick in Game 4 and added a fourth goal in the series in the Game 6 clincher.

Awaiting the Cinderella North Stars in the Stanley Cup Final were the defending-champion New York Islanders. Ciccarelli posted 3 goals and 2 assists in the series, but the clock struck midnight on Minnesota's fairytale run, and the North Stars fell in five games.

Ciccarelli's consolation was a permanent spot in the NHL and rookie playoff records, with 14 goals

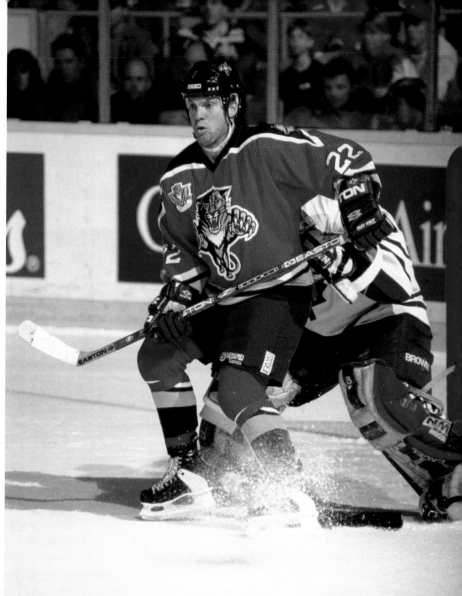

and 21 points. The points record has since been equaled by Ville Leino of the Philadelphia Flyers in 2010, but still no rookie has scored more than 11 goals in the playoffs.

Ciccarelli's first full NHL season ended up being the best of his career. He set career highs in goals (55) and points (106) in 1981–82, marking his first of seven seasons of 30 or more goals — including two over 50 — in Minnesota. In nine seasons with the North Stars, he scored 332 goals and 651 points in 602 games.

After stints with Washington, Detroit, Tampa Bay and Florida, the player no one chose to draft had played 1,232 regular-season games, scored 608 goals and added 592 assists for an even 1,200 points. In 141 playoff games, he added 73 goals and 118 points.

The majority of those goals were scored within a stick's length of the net, and he absorbed a lot of opponents' lumber to earn them. He was also known

to use his own, amassing 1,425 minutes in penalties, including a 10-game suspension and a day in jail for clubbing the Toronto Maple Leafs' Luke Richardson over the head with his stick in 1988.

The incident may have delayed induction, but Ciccarelli was welcomed to the Hall of Fame in 2010 in his eighth year of eligibility.

His dad died before he could see his son in the Hall of Fame, but Ciccarelli says that two of his favorite moments in hockey were having him there when he scored his 500th and 600th career goals.

As for the magical playoff run and record, Ciccarelli describes the alchemy of it as the "right time, right place, right team.

"Lou Nanne gave me an opportunity, put me with Tom McCarthy and Neal Broten. We gelled … It was a great experience.

"It's nice [the rookie record is] still there."

# MARCEL DIONNE

## The Last Scoring Champ Before Gretzky's Remarkable Run

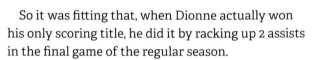

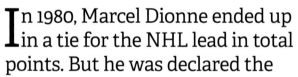

In 1980, Marcel Dionne ended up in a tie for the NHL lead in total points. But he was declared the winner of the Art Ross Trophy because he had scored two more goals than the other guy. He admits to experiencing mixed emotions about it all.

"In the back of my mind I was thinking, 'I consider that it's a tie because I believe assists are just as important,'" Dionne recalls. "'But I guess that's the rule, so I won it. But geez, it's going to be 10 years before anyone else wins it again, so I'm glad I won it now.'"

Dionne's mental calculation was not far off. It would take eight seasons before Mario Lemieux wrestled the NHL scoring crown from the head of Wayne Gretzky, who had tied Dionne in 1979–80 with 137 points. Gretzky went on to win the scoring race in 10 of the next 14 seasons.

"But as far as I'm concerned, we tied for the scoring title," Dionne insists. "Sometimes making an assist meant a lot more than scoring itself. I remember many times breaking out 2-on-none, and I always had the greatest satisfaction in giving the other guy the puck for a chance to score.

"You teach kids a passing play is as good as scoring goals."

So it was fitting that, when Dionne actually won his only scoring title, he did it by racking up 2 assists in the final game of the regular season.

Dionne, whose 731 career regular-season goals trail only those of Gretzky, Gordie Howe, Brett Hull and Jaromir Jagr on the all-time list, scored 53 goals and had 84 assists. Gretzky, making his NHL debut a year after turning pro in the World Hockey Association, which merged with the NHL in the summer of 1979, had 51 goals and 86 assists.

It was Dionne's second 50-goal season and kicked off a string of five straight years in which he went 50 or higher.

The goal that gave Dionne the Art Ross came at 4:15 of the first period of a 4–1 win over Quebec in the seventh-to-last game of the schedule. The insurance marker came two nights later against the Colorado Rockies.

Dionne's pursuit of the title was ably assisted by his mates on the Los Angeles Kings' Triple Crown line. Over the 1979–80 and 1980–81 seasons, Dionne and his wingers, Charlie Simmer and Dave Taylor,

averaged 112 points each, and in 1980–81 they became the first forward unit to each record 100 or more points.

Dionne still appreciates the fact that he played on a three-man line, compared to the modern practice of two simpatico players teamed with a rotating third man.

"That was really significant in the '50s and '60s and early '70s," Dionne recalled to NHL.com. "You had a unit that played [together] a lot. As a unit, I look at the Islanders, like [Mike] Bossy, [Bryan] Trottier and Clark Gillies. You look at the French Connection with René Robert, [Gilbert] Perreault and [Rick] Martin. People love that.

"To have a successful line, you've got to get along together and respond together. That's what we had. We had a lot of chemistry.

"The rest was just poetry on the ice; it was unbelievable: tremendous effort, a lot of goals, a lot of points, a lot of puck control, which you don't have today — it's puck-chasing."

Despite the exploits of the Triple Crown line, the Kings were defeated in the opening round of the playoffs four straight years. In 1980 it was a 3–1 loss to the Cup-bound New York Islanders, who had finished 17 points ahead of them in the standings.

Because the Kings didn't win a league or conference championship in his time, Dionne is sometimes overlooked when fans list the top players of all time, even though he ranks fifth in career goals and sixth in points.

"My idea was simple. Put it on net, anywhere, any time. Most of the time, I tried to do the screen shot and use the defenseman. Our defensemen stood up more than they do today.

"And you have to be patient, move the puck to get the shot."

While he considered the assist just as important, Dionne enjoyed every one of his 700-plus goals.

"I never thought it was boring to score a goal," he says, adding with a laugh, "but it was not like today, when guys act like they've never scored before. But I guess they don't score as often now."

# PHIL ESPOSITO

## Taking Scoring to a New Level

I n 1967 when Phil Esposito was told he'd been traded to the Boston Bruins from the Chicago Black Hawks — going from first to worst in the NHL — he considered calling it quits. He was only 25, but the steel plant in his hometown of Sault Ste. Marie, Ontario, where he worked during the NHL off-season, paid as well and offered a more secure future.

Growing up, Esposito acquired a reputation that stuck with him in Chicago: he was too mouthy, too slow, too fat and having too much fun away from the rink. That reputation cost him a spot on midget and junior teams and led to his trade to Boston. But whenever he was on the ice, he put up points and put the puck in the net.

Once he decided to report to the Bruins' training camp, coaches parked Esposito in the slot, where his wingers could feed him the puck. His 6-foot-1, 205-pound body would absorb punishment while he deflected shots or scored on rebounds. He became "the highest paid garbage collector in the United States," as hockey writer Stan Fischler put it.

"Scoring is easy," Esposito later said. "You simply stand in the slot, take your beating and shoot the puck into the net."

Despite Fischler's quip, Esposito was making only $8,000 a year when he went to the Bruins. They refused his contract demand of $12,000 but agreed to pay him bonuses for hitting a series of scoring targets.

It was a wise negotiation by Esposito. In his second game as a Bruin, he scored 4 goals — 3 on the power play — and in his first year in Boston, he led the NHL in assists.

In 1968–69, Esposito became the first NHL player with more than 100 points. He had 126 points, including 49 goals, shattering the record of 97 points shared by Chicago teammates Stan Mikita and Bobby Hull — his old playing and drinking partner.

The following year Esposito had 99 points, and he

On a rebound, Esposito beat Kings goalie Denis DeJordy — a former Chicago teammate — to become the NHL's greatest goal-scorer.

"I saw Green take the shot, and I know Teddy shoots low," described Esposito after the game. "I knew I could score if I could get my stick on it. I've played with DeJordy, and I thought I could beat him."

There was little fanfare, however. "I celebrated the goal the same as I did any other goal," said Esposito years later.

Esposito also scored his 60th goal that night, surpassing the total of 59 that Montreal Canadiens legend Jean Béliveau had scored in the regular season *and* playoffs in 1955–56. The two goals gave him 128 points on the season, breaking his own record set just two years earlier.

"I'm glad it's over," said Esposito after the Bruins won 7–2, making them the first team in NHL history to win 50 games in a season.

"With 11 games after this one, I knew sooner or later I'd get it. But I've been fortunate against Los Angeles, and I like playing here. I'm just glad the pressure's off."

Esposito went on to score 16 goals in those 11 games, finishing the 78-game season with 76 goals and 76 assists for 152 points. He also set a record with 550 shots in the season — only one player has since come within 100 shots of that number.

With the bonuses he earned by scoring 76 goals, Esposito finally quit Algoma Steel for good.

The Bruins had the top-4 scorers in the NHL in 1970–71, led by Esposito, who credits his teammates for his success that year.

"I could never have broken the record without my teammates," says Esposito. "From Bobby Orr to [John] McKenzie, from Hodge to Cashman, from [Johnny] Bucyk to [Gerry] Cheevers. Without them, I couldn't have done it in a million years."

The group was incredibly close. "Was this really a team," asked the *Boston Globe*'s Kevin Paul Dupont, "or some sort of brotherhood that had come together years after signing a blood oath in the backwoods of Canada?"

One of the legends of Beantown is that teammates — led by Orr in hospital scrubs — wheeled Esposito's gurney out of Massachusetts General and through the snowy streets of Boston after he had knee surgery in 1973. They ended up at Orr's bar, the Branding Iron.

scored 13 goals and 27 points in 14 playoff games as the Bruins ended a 29-year Stanley Cup drought in May 1970. The Bruins had gone from the NHL basement to the penthouse, with a swagger that started with their leading scorer.

And in 1970–71, with the help of wingers Ken Hodge and Wayne Cashman, Esposito took scoring to heights previously unimaginable.

On March 10 he tied Hull's single-season record of 58 goals, in an 8–1 win over the California Golden Seals. The next night the Bruins were in Los Angeles to play the Kings.

Hockey hadn't captured the imagination of the Golden State, and "there was relatively nobody in the building for the game," according to Esposito, despite the attractions of the NHL's resident powerhouse team and a record on the verge of being broken.

"Doc, don't worry, we are handling Phil just like a baby," said Orr over the phone when the surgeon tracked him down. "He's having a beer, and we will have him back in 15 minutes."

After his record-setting campaign, Esposito had three more years with more than 60 goals before the rebuilding Bruins dealt him to the New York Rangers early in the 1975–76 season.

As a Bruin, Esposito had won five scoring titles, led the NHL in goals for six straight seasons, won the Hart Trophy twice, won the Lester Pearson Trophy for league MVP as chosen by the players and won the Lester Patrick Trophy for his contribution to hockey in the United States.

Esposito finished his career on Broadway in January 1981, halfway through his 18th season. "I started losing my enthusiasm," he admitted.

"Seven goals in 40 games — that's not Phil Esposito," said Carol Vadnais, who had been traded to the Rangers with Esposito. "The defense was checking him as hard; they were checking him as if he were 28 years old. But he was 38."

With 717 career goals and 1,590 points, Esposito trailed only Gordie Howe in both categories when he walked away.

The season Esposito retired, Wayne Gretzky broke his single-season points record, with 164, and in 1981–82 he set the new mark for goals, with 92. Esposito was in Buffalo to present Gretzky with the puck he used to score his 77th goal.

Afterwards, a relieved Gretzky said, "It took the pressure off me. Now Phil can stop following me around and get back to his business."

Esposito entered the Hall of Fame in 1984, but his heart was still in Boston: "I don't care [about being inducted into] the Hall of Fame, to tell you the truth. My biggest thrill was having my number retired at Boston Garden. That to me is where it's at."

Esposito, who quit Catholic school in Grade 12 to pursue his hockey dream, inspired the bumper sticker popular in Boston in the 1970s: "Jesus saves — and Esposito puts in the rebound."

# RON FRANCIS

## The Quiet Difference Maker

Ron Francis might be the most underappreciated and unsung superstar in NHL history.

"I heard it put once that it is probably the quietest 1,500-plus points that anybody has ever scored," said Francis after he passed boyhood hero Phil Esposito in 2001 for fifth on the all-time scoring list, 20 years after he was drafted fourth overall by the Hartford Whalers.

"That's probably true. But it doesn't really matter to me what people say about me. As individuals you try to go out there and work as hard as you possibly can, and at the end of the day, you can look in the mirror and know that you've tried your best and given everything you have. That's when you have to be satisfied. That's all I've ever been concerned with."

Francis certainly gave his all to the Whalers. Called up partway through the 1981–82 season, he had 68 points in 59 games. It was the team's third season in the NHL, and over the next nine years, Francis became the face of the franchise as he dragged them to respectability. He led the team in scoring and to the playoffs five times before he was traded to the Pittsburgh Penguins in 1991.

In Pittsburgh, on a team with Mario Lemieux and Jaromir Jagr — not to mention legends and multiple-Cup winners like Bryan Trottier and Paul Coffey — Francis didn't have to bear the burden of carrying the offense. But he quietly and naturally became a respected leader.

"He was a true professional, on and off the ice," says Mark Recchi. "He's a better person than he was a player — and he was a great player."

The Penguins won their first Stanley Cup later that year. "Coffey knew all about winning Cups, and he told me to enjoy the moment, but that it would get better every day the rest of my life," Francis said of the immediate aftermath of the title. "He was right."

The 1991–92 season started with a Stanley Cup hangover and the loss of beloved head coach "Badger" Bob Johnson to a brain tumor. The Penguins finished third in their division, and when the 1992 playoffs started, Francis was playing on a badly injured knee he suffered late in the season. "I didn't think [my knee] was going to make it through the Washington series," he says. "But when you're winning hockey games, you don't feel it as much. And

when you see the finish line ahead of you, it gives you the incentive to just play through."

In Game 4 of the Patrick Division final against the New York Rangers, the Penguins were trailing two games to one in the series and 3–1 in the game when a Francis shot from his own blue line beat Rangers goalie Mike Richter at 19:54 of the second period.

Francis scored another in the third period and got his sixth of the series at 2:47 into overtime to complete the hat trick and tie the series.

"I've never heard the arena that loud," recalled teammate Phil Bourque. "Ronnie Francis — that's what I remember from the series. That overtime goal for the hat trick was the stuff of legend."

That was the start of seven straight Pittsburgh wins, including a sweep of the Boston Bruins in the conference final to set up a Stanley Cup matchup against the Chicago Blackhawks.

The Penguins' winning streak reached 11 as they swept Chicago for their second consecutive Cup, and it was Francis' 8th goal of the playoffs that held up as the Cup winner in a wild 6–5 final in Game 4. The goal was Francis' 27th point in 19 playoff games.

Francis racked up 723 points in 533 games for Pittsburgh and 100 points in 97 playoff games. In 1994–95

he became the first player in history to win the Selke Trophy as the NHL's best defensive forward and the Lady Byng as the league's most gentlemanly player. He had a career-high 119 points in 1995–96, including a league-leading 92 assists.

Francis returned to the Whalers as a free agent in 1998. In his absence the team had relocated to Carolina and become the Hurricanes, and 10 years after clinching the Cup for the Penguins, Francis, at the age of 39, led the Hurricanes in scoring and a surprise run to the Stanley Cup Final. Carolina lost the championship, but Francis did win his third Lady Byng that year and added the King Clancy Memorial Trophy as the player who best exemplifies leadership qualities on and off the ice.

When he retired after 23 NHL seasons, Francis had played the third-most games in NHL history (1,731), scored the fourth-most points (1,798 on 549 goals and 1,249 assists), and was second in career assists to Wayne Gretzky's 1,963. Perhaps most impressive: he scored 20 or more goals in 20 seasons, a total surpassed only by Gordie Howe, with 22.

"Just a class guy," says former Pittsburgh teammate Kevin Stevens. "We would have never won the Stanley Cup without him."

# MIKE GARTNER

## Making 30 the New Normal

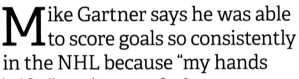ike Gartner says he was able to score goals so consistently in the NHL because "my hands had finally caught up to my feet."

And what feet. Gartner set a long-standing record for the fastest time in the NHL skills competition and was acclaimed throughout his career for constantly outracing his check down the right side of the ice. When he retired in 1998, he held the records for most seasons with 30 goals (17 of them, a record that still stands) and most consecutive 30-goal seasons (15, a mark since tied by Jaromir Jagr). From his first NHL season with the Washington Capitals to his 18th and penultimate season with the Phoenix Coyotes, the only time he did not hit 30 goals was in the lockout-shortened 1994–95 season, when each team played only 48 games, of which he played just 38.

Another key to his offensive consistency was a knack for staying off the injured list. "I stayed relatively healthy throughout my career, and before you know it, I was in my 9th, 10th, 11th season, and somebody said, 'That's your 10th year in a row in which you've scored 30 goals. Do you know the record is 13?'" he told the Hockey Hall of Fame. "I didn't know it at the time. I was given a certain amount of talent, and I wanted to do the best I could every time I stepped onto the ice. I really strived for that consistency, and as a result, I was able to have it."

After playing for Cincinnati in the World Hockey Association's final year, during which he scored "only" 27 times as a 19-year-old playing on a line with fellow teenager Mark Messier, Gartner was drafted fourth overall by Washington. He soon developed an improved scoring touch, notching 84 goals in his first two NHL seasons. He credits the scoring surge to the opportunities provided by the Capitals.

Gartner reached the 30-goal plateau for the 17th and final time on March 6, 1997, in the Coyotes' 5–0 road victory over the Tampa Bay Lightning. He scored the 30th against Rick Tabaracci and his 31st against Corey Schwab — one on a power play, the other at even strength.

His marker against Tabaracci, at 9:46 of the second period, cinched his 17th 30-goal season in 17 full-schedule years, and then he hit the 1,300-point mark of his career with his goal against Schwab early in

the third period. The night before he had netted number 29 by redirecting Craig Janney's power-play shot in a 3–0 win over goalie John Vanbiesbrouck and the Florida Panthers. The back-to-back victories in the state of Florida moved Phoenix a game over .500 in their first season out of Winnipeg and helped ensure they would make the playoffs.

Gartner, traded to Phoenix from Toronto in the off-season, was no stranger to landmark lamplighters. He scored the first goal for the new franchise in the team's second game as the Coyotes, recording Phoenix's first-ever hat track in the same game. He also scored the last goal in the Chicago Stadium and was the first NHLer to record his 500th goal, 500th assist and 1,000th point in the same season.

Gartner's inclusion in the Hockey Hall of Fame has been questioned in some quarters, but not among those who really know the game. He retired as the second-highest goal-scoring right-winger and fifth overall goal-scorer in NHL history, with 708 goals. He is fourth all time in right-wing scoring, more than balancing out the fact that he scored 50 goals in a season only once and didn't play in a Stanley Cup Final, make an all-star team or win an individual league award. But few players have shown his propensity for regularly delivering a goal total that still holds cachet: 30 in a season.

"Thirty goals is something I've always looked at as a real minimum for a goal-scorer," he said right after he put his 17th such campaign to bed.

He set that high bar early in his career and kept clearing it year after year.

# MICHEL GOULET

## Right Place, Right Time

$I$t is a record that, until the spring of 2016, Michel Goulet didn't know he shared.

"Really?" the Hall of Fame left-winger said when told that he and Phil Esposito, who did it twice, are the only players in NHL history to score 16 game-winning goals in a single season. "It's something I've never thought too much about. The stats were nothing back then like they are today."

"Back then" was the 1983–84 season, the Quebec Nordiques' fifth in the NHL after the league expanded in 1979 to absorb Quebec, Edmonton, Winnipeg and Hartford, the four surviving World Hockey Association franchises. Goulet, who had played in Quebec City as a junior and in Birmingham as an underage 18-year-old in the WHA, was one of the centerpieces of the entertaining, puck-moving Nordiques. Quebec considered him a must-get in the 1979 amateur draft — a draft that, because of the abundance of young WHA talent, is regularly acknowledged as the strongest and deepest in NHL history.

Although the Nordiques drafted late, at 20th overall, they were able to land Goulet because of a clause in his Birmingham contract that stipulated if the team folded, Quebec had to be offered his rights

ahead of any other NHL team. Goulet's agent obtained a court order to enforce the clause, and that scared off the teams selecting earlier in the first round.

One of the reasons Goulet didn't know he shares the record for game-winning goals is that he placed every one of his 548 regular-season goals in high regard.

"I don't really have a favorite," he explains. "To me, goals are special. I didn't win the Cup, but there were still goals that could make a difference. I remember having 4 against Montreal one time, and that was special because of the intense rivalry.

"There is no question that playing on the top two lines, you wanted to be a guy who made a difference, and I tried to play as a player who could make an impact.

"I'm no Wayne Gretzky, I'm no Mario Lemieux. The thing I tried to do as much as score goals was to be

consistent year after year. I didn't try to just score goals; I wanted to be a playmaker too."

With that many game-winners, it would be natural to assume that Goulet was being set up by Peter Stastny, which was certainly true in some power-play situations.

"But Dale Hunter was my regular center," he points out. "We played together for seven years. As we all know, we didn't have too many right-handed shots playing center in those days [Hunter shot left], so the left wing was always the back-checker."

Which makes Goulet's scoring prowess all the more impressive. Goulet ranked second in goals in 1983–84, with 56, and more than a quarter of them were game-winners. He made the NHL First All-Star Team while helping the Nordiques to a franchise-record 34 wins, although Quebec could not get past their bitter archrival, Montreal, in the second round of the playoffs, which the Canadiens won in six games. It was one of four consecutive 50-goal seasons for Goulet, who at 23 became the second-youngest player (behind 20-year-old Gretzky) among the top-10 leading scorers of game-winning goals in a season.

There is a running debate as to whether a game-winning goal should be the one that puts a team ahead to stay (as in soccer) or, as the NHL defines the term, the goal that in hindsight gives the winning team one more goal than the losing team's total. The latter is, properly, the goal that ensures victory.

"Sometimes it's the goal that made the difference, and sometimes it's the third goal in a 6–2 game," Goulet shrugs.

In his 15 other NHL and WHA seasons, Goulet was never credited with more than six game-winners.

"Sometimes I think these things just happen," he said. "It's a lot about being in the right place at the right time."

Goulet has said, only half-jokingly, that he might have scored 100 goals in a season if he had played on Gretzky's line. Gretzky was his center in the 1984 Canada Cup, and three years later Goulet was often overlooked as a rotating third member of a line that also boasted Gretzky and Mario Lemieux in the fabulously entertaining 1987 Canada Cup.

"My biggest goals were the 2 against Sweden in the '84 Canada Cup. But to me, goals are special, all goals.

"A goal is a goal."

# WAYNE GRETZKY

## 50 Goals in
## 39 Games

W ith his slight physique and feathered hair, 18-year-old Wayne Gretzky looked at least as much like a kid hanging around in front of the corner store bumming smokes, in his hometown of Brantford, as a prospect on the cusp of stepping into the NHL in 1979. Yet two years later, he set one of the most unbreakable records in NHL history.

The transition to the big stage turned out to be an easy one for the scoring sensation, who had been in the public eye since before puberty. Gretzky tied for the NHL scoring lead in his rookie year, but the Art Ross Trophy was awarded to Marcel Dionne because he had 53 goals to Gretzky's 51. That went against Walter Gretzky's early lesson that an assist is just as good as a goal — advice his son took to heart, developing extrasensory passing skills.

"Everyone will tell you, 'Oh yeah, I saw it right away. He was a genius on the ice.' They're lying," says Tom McVie, who coached against the Edmonton Oilers in the World Hockey Association and NHL, of the young Gretzky. "To me, he looked like somebody's little brother. It looked like he was going to get killed. But he made one pass that season that made me stop and think. He was behind the net with two guys, and

he made this back pass to Blair MacDonald. I remember thinking, 'How did he know he was there?'"

Gretzky won the Hart Trophy as league MVP in his first NHL season and kept it in his sophomore year, in which he scored 55 goals and won the Art Ross outright. NHL defensemen had made a Faustian bargain by then, letting him shoot because his distribution of the puck was so deadly.

Ever-evolving, in his third season Gretzky took what his opponents gave him.

"I don't think anyone had to tell him to shoot more," says former teammate Kevin Lowe. "I think that teams may have started to pay more attention to covering his wings and left him alone. And one thing about Wayne: he always made the right play."

Living his own mantra that you miss 100 percent of the shots you don't take, Gretzky was on pace to reach the gold standard — or should that be "goal standard"? — set by the Montreal Canadiens' Maurice Richard in 1944–45: the symmetrical feat of 50 goals in 50 games. The Rocket's pace went un-

matched for 36 years, until Mike Bossy of the New York Islanders scored his 50th goal in the Islanders' 50th game on January 24, 1981.

On Halloween 1981, Gretzky scored 4 goals in the Oilers' 13th game, a night he credits with igniting his momentous season. It was the first of four games that season in which he scored at least 4 goals — a modern NHL record, matched only once: by Gretzky himself, two seasons later.

In late November he scored his 31st goal early in game 26. It was his 7th goal in seven periods, but then he went cold. Over the next four games, he was goal-less.

Gretzky scored a single goal in each of the following four games to give him 35 goals in 34 contests. With Gretzky still on pace to match Richard and Bossy, fans were starting to think about getting tickets for game 50 in late January.

Then the Oilers headed home for a five-game engagement around Christmastime, and what a wonderful gift Gretzky had for Edmonton. On

December 19, he had 3 goals and 7 points in a win over the Minnesota North Stars. The next night, he scored twice in a loss to the Calgary Flames. On December 23 he added a goal as the Oilers beat the Vancouver Canucks, putting him at 41 goals in 37 games.

Then came the Oilers whopping 10–5 win over the Los Angeles Kings on December 27, in which Gretzky had another four-goal game. In four games at the Northlands Coliseum, he had 10 goals and 19 points, and with 45 goals in 38 games, the Richard-Bossy milestone seemed inevitable, if a few games away.

"I thought to myself, 'You can't choke now,'" said Gretzky.

The fifth game of the homestand was on December 30 against a strong Philadelphia Flyers team backed by goalie Pete Peeters. Gretzky, though, started early, with a little luck.

"Charlie Huddy took a shot from the left point that bounced off the boards and right to me at the corner of the net, and I put it in. I thought to myself, 'How fortunate.'"

It was that kind of night. Later in the first period, he finished a 4-on-2, surprising Peeters with a shot from 20 feet out. In the second, he earned his hat trick by splitting the Flyers defense and firing home a slap shot. In the third, he hit goal 49 after cutting to the middle and slapping another over Peeters' shoulder.

History and highlights show Peeters as the victim, but he also robbed the red-hot scorer on several occasions. "I had eight or nine good chances," remembers Gretzky. "Their goalie made some terrific saves."

With the Oilers leading 6–5, Peeters went off for an extra attacker. Gretzky sealed the 7–5 win and a place in history with three seconds left in the game. The empty-netter was assisted by goalie Grant Fuhr and Glenn Anderson, as Bill Barber dove to block it.

"Bill Barber said that if I were going in alone on an empty net for the 50th goal, he'd throw his stick [which results in an automatic goal]," says Gretzky. "That would have made a great trivia question: how I scored my 50th goal without putting the puck into the net."

Gretzky had scored 9 goals in two games — the only time in modern NHL history a player has had back-to-back games with at least four goals — to reach 50 in only 39 games.

After witnessing Gretzky's historic game up close, Flyer great and fellow Hall of Famer Bobby Clarke said, "I know everything that's been written about you. I think none of it is adequate."

Gretzky was held off the score sheet in his next game but had 11 goals in the next 11 games to hit 61 in 50 games, which also remains a record. On February 24, 1982, he broke Phil Esposito's single-season goal record of 76, scoring goals 77, 78 and 79 in the last seven minutes of the game. The natural hat trick continued a streak of four consecutive 5-point games, as he surpassed Esposito with six weeks still left in the season.

Gretzky finished the year with 92, but, even with a record that still stands and seems ironclad, it didn't quite meet his standards.

"It was a thrill to get 92 goals, but in some ways, I thought I let myself down by not getting 100," reminisced Gretzky 30 years later. "Maybe I should have pushed myself more."

Gretzky had 10 hat tricks in 1981–82, and, living up to his father Walter's wise words, in each of those games he added enough assists to give him at least 5 points. With 120 assists, his 212 total points obliterated the record of 164 he had set the year before, which in turn had broken Esposito's old mark of 152, set in 1970–71. It was the first of four seasons in which Gretzky had at least 200 points. No other player has ever done that.

The scrawny kid who grew up to be the greatest scorer in hockey history would retire with more than 60 official NHL records to his name, along with a host of accomplishments that don't appear in the league's *Official Guide & Record Book*. The one that matters most to him is the one least likely to be equaled.

"People ask me all the time about my records, but to me, that's my favorite," says Gretzky about his 50 goals in 39 games. "They're all made to be broken; that's what sports is.

"That's what's so great about sports, but that's my favorite because I think that will be the hardest to break."

# DALE HAWERCHUK

## Rookie Record Kick-Starts Jets Turnaround

Like many boys his age, Dale Hawerchuk's idol was Bobby Orr, the offensively gifted Boston Bruins All-Star defenseman who first turned heads as an underage player in the Ontario Hockey League with the Oshawa Generals.

Hawerchuk too was turning heads at a young age, scoring all 8 goals in the final of a prestigious Montreal peewee tournament, breaking a record for goals in a game, first set by Guy Lafleur.

When Hawerchuk was 15, the Oshawa Generals — Orr's former club — offered him a try-out. He didn't make the team, and the Generals assigned him to their Junior B affiliate, coached by the legendary future NHL and Team Canada coach Mike Keenan. He did well enough there that the Quebec Major Junior Hockey League's (QMJHL) Cornwall Royals (who, despite being in the Quebec league, were able to select players in Ontario) drafted him sixth overall in 1979. "I wondered if they were a new team in the OHL," says Hawerchuk. "I knew nothing about them."

And like his idol before him, Hawerchuk's major junior debut was stellar, scoring 103 points and winning the QMJHL Rookie of the Year. He added a whopping 45 points in 18 games in the playoffs as the team captured the Memorial Cup.

At the time, the Memorial Cup winner represented Canada at the World Junior Championship, and Hawerchuk tied for the tournament lead with 9 points.

In his second season in Cornwall, "all the pressure was on [Hawerchuk]" according to fellow Royal and future Hall of Famer Doug Gilmour. "It would be like [Connor] McDavid now or [Sidney] Crosby in his junior years. Dale came through with flying colors."

Hawerchuk had 81 goals and 183 points, won Canadian Major Junior Player of the Year and was named Memorial Cup MVP as the Royals repeated.

The NHL draft in 1981 was a no-brainer: the Winni-

Hawerchuk played every game that season, scoring 45 goals and 103 points. He broke 17 franchise records, including points in a season, and was the youngest player to ever be named the NHL's top rookie.

Hawerchuk was also the youngest player in history to have more than 100 points and the first rookie to have 40 goals and 100 points in the same season — the second-highest point total ever recorded by an NHL freshman.

That record was owned by Wayne Gretzky, who was two years older and two provinces over, in the city of Edmonton. The two shared a work ethic and a certain style of play; neither appeared to be the smoothest or quickest skater, but they just kept scoring.

*Goal* magazine called Hawerchuk "Mini-Gretzky," and Mike Doran, the Winnipeg Jets' director of player personnel when Hawerchuk was drafted, said, "He has the same instincts — that puck sense — of Gretzky."

In 1984–85, Hawerchuk had 53 goals and 130 points — both career highs — and he finished second in Hart Trophy voting. No prizes for guessing the winner.

Playing alongside Gretzky in the historic 1987 Canada Cup, Hawerchuk scored the fifth goal in the deciding game of the final against the Soviet Union and won the faceoff that led to the Gretzky-to-Lemieux, tournament-winning sixth goal.

In 1990, Hawerchuk was traded to the Buffalo Sabres. He had scored 379 goals in 713 games with the Jets. It took 1,422 games over 20 seasons for Shane Doan to break Hawerchuk's Jets/Phoenix Coyotes franchise record (which Doan did, fittingly, against the new incarnation of the Winnipeg Jets).

Hawerchuk spent five years with the Sabres before closing out his career in St. Louis and Philadelphia, becoming the first NHLer to play 1,000 games before his 31st birthday.

Hawerchuk retired in 1997 after losing in the Stanley Cup Final with the Flyers, the first final of his career. He left the game with 518 goals and 1,409 points in 1,188 career games, and was inducted into the Hall of Fame in 2001.

"People think because you are in the Hall of Fame it must have been easy for you, but that was not the case with me," said Hawerchuk in 2015. "I could get results, but I wasn't the greatest skater. I had to find a way to score."

peg Jets picked Hawerchuk first overall and introduced him with great fanfare on August 13.

Hawerchuk was driven to the Jets' 10th anniversary party on the corner of Portage and Main in downtown Winnipeg in a Brinks truck. When he arrived he signed his first pro contract and was handed the No. 10 jersey while the mayor and members of the provincial legislature looked on.

It was a lot of hype for a shy teen to live up to, but fans and dignitaries would not be disappointed. In 1981–82, 18-year-old Hawerchuk led the Jets to the single biggest turnaround by any team in NHL history. After just nine wins the season prior, the Jets won 33 games and had 80 points — a 48-point improvement.

# GORDIE HOWE

## Breaking the Rocket's Record

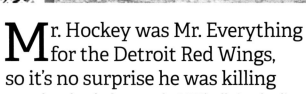

**M**r. Hockey was Mr. Everything for the Detroit Red Wings, so it's no surprise he was killing a penalty when he became the NHL's all-time leading goal-scorer.

On October 27, 1963, Gordie Howe scored the 544th goal of his career, against Gump Worsley in a 6–4 loss to the Canadiens. In doing so, he tied the record set by Maurice "Rocket" Richard — the man Howe knocked out with one punch the first time he played the Canadiens in Montreal — who had retired three years earlier.

But then Howe went cold, going five games without a goal.

"Looking back at the chase for number 545, I know now that I was far too deep into my own head," wrote Howe in his autobiography *Mr. Hockey*. "As the slump went on, I started thinking about all the things I knew about putting the puck in the net. I even thought back to playing goalie as a kid."

Howe was the sixth of nine children growing up on a farm in Saskatchewan. He started his hockey career in net before moving up to defense and finally to forward. At 15 he tried out for the New York Rangers but left camp early because he was homesick.

A year later he made an impression on Detroit coach and general manager Jack Adams in a tryout with the Red Wings in Windsor, Ontario. Impressed with Howe's ambidexterity — he scored a goal shooting left and another from the right side — Adams signed him, and two years later in 1946, Howe made his NHL debut.

After his first NHL game, the *Detroit News* wrote: "Gordon Howe is the squad's baby, 18 years old. But he was one of Detroit's most valuable men last night. In his first major league game, he scored a goal, skated tirelessly and had perfect poise. The goal came when he literally powered his way through the players from the blue line to the goalmouth."

That power was a sign of things to come — Howe elbowed his way to the top as one of the toughest players of his era — but the goal wasn't. He scored just seven times in his first season and had only 35 goals in his first three years in the league.

In his first All-Star Game, in 1948, Howe got a five-minute penalty for fighting. Once he learned to stay out of the penalty box, however, he managed at least

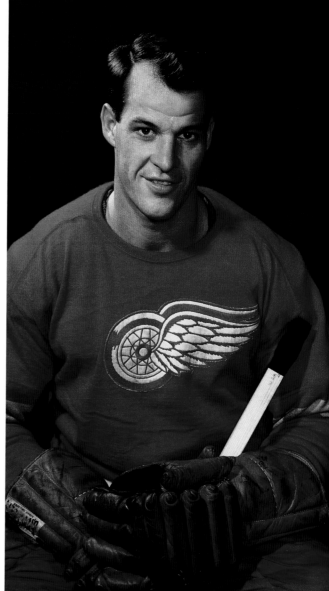

20 goals every season for the next three decades.

In 1949–50, the Production line of Howe, Sid Abel and Ted Lindsay claimed the top three spots in the NHL scoring race. Against the Toronto Maple Leafs in the first game of the playoffs that year, Howe missed a check on Ted Kennedy and crashed head-first into the boards. Unconscious with a fractured skull, he was rushed to the hospital, where a doctor drilled into his skull to relieve the pressure.

He was in critical condition and was told he'd never play again, but the following season, with a soft spot on his head and a facial tic, Howe led the NHL with 86 points — 20 more than runner-up Richard. His 43 goals were one more than Richard's and earned him the first of five goal-scoring titles.

By 1963 — in his 18th season — Howe had more points (1,220) and assists (676) than anyone in NHL history, and he was bearing down on Richard's goal-scoring record when he started to overthink and lose sight of his game.

"What I wasn't doing at the time, though, was remembering to see what the puck sees," said Howe. "Doing that allows you to simply take what's given to you. That's how I got number 545."

On November 10 the Red Wings were playing the Canadiens again, and at 15:06 of the second period, Howe took a pass from Billy McNeill and beat goalie Charlie Hodge low between the post and his right pad for a shorthanded goal.

"All I remember is the puck going plunk," said Howe after the 3–0 win. "Now I can start enjoying life again."

The biggest crowd of the year at the Olympia — 15,027, with 3,000 more turned away at the gate — gave Howe an ovation that lasted more than 10 minutes.

"I don't know what felt better: the outpouring of appreciation from thousands of fans or the relief of getting the monkey off my back. Either way it was a moment I'll never forget. With the big goal out of the way, I also knew my teammates would stop walking on eggshells around me. They'd been treating me like I was a starting pitcher going for a no-hitter."

Howe wasn't close to finished. In 1969 he scored his 715th goal, which was newsworthy in the United States because he had surpassed Babe Ruth's home run total. When he retired for the first time in 1971, after 25 seasons in Detroit, the runners-up on the all-time scoring list were far behind in his rearview mirror. His 786 goals were 232 more than Bobby Hull, his 1,023 assists were 300 ahead of Alex Delvecchio, and with 1,809 points, he had a whopping 590 more than Jean Béliveau.

Writer Mordecai Richler called Howe "the man for whom time had stopped," and the ageless wonder returned with the Houston Aeros of the World Hockey Association (WHA) in 1973 so he could play with sons Mark and Marty. In 1974 at the age of 46, he led the WHA in scoring, with 100 points, and was named league MVP.

After the WHA merged with the NHL in 1979, the 51-year-old Howe played all 80 games for the Hartford Whalers before retiring for good in 1980. "This man could run up Mount Everest," the team cardiologist said before the right-winger's final season.

Howe was in the top 5 in NHL scoring in 20 straight seasons (1949–50 through 1968–69), was named to the first All-Star Team 12 times and to the Second Team nine more, and he won six Art Ross Trophies, six Hart Trophies and four Stanley Cups.

Howe's final NHL tally was 1,767 games played, 801 goals scored and 1,850 points — not to mention 1,685 penalty minutes — in a career that started the year after World War II ended.

Named to the 1980 All-Star Game in Detroit by coach Scotty Bowman, 32 years after his first All-Star Game, Howe played against 19-year-old rookie Wayne Gretzky. The kid who grew up idolizing Howe would eventually break his record for goals.

"As much as I enjoyed holding down the top spot, I knew it wouldn't last forever," wrote Howe in *Mr. Hockey*.

"You don't get called 'the Great One' unless you're something special, and Wayne, it goes without saying, was a once-in-a-generation talent. Watching his artistry on the ice was a treat for everyone who loves the game of hockey. If anyone had to bump me down the ladder, I'm happy that it was him. As I've always said since then, the way I see it, the record is in good hands."

The NHL record, at least. With their WHA tallies included, Howe had 975 goals to Gretzky's 931.

It's a record that may last forever — just as the career of the tireless skater, who on some nights played 45 minutes, seemed to do.

# BOBBY HULL

## The First Past the Half-Century Mark

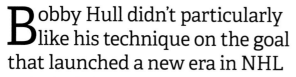

Bobby Hull didn't particularly like his technique on the goal that launched a new era in NHL scoring, but he loved the result.

"I moved the puck out front for the slap shot. I got it out too far and almost topped it — didn't get real good wood on the thing, and it skidded away, skimming the ice," Hull recalled of his 51st goal of the 1965–66 season, when he became the first player to surpass the 50-goal single-season mark he'd shared with Rocket Richard and Bernie "Boom-Boom" Geoffrion. "I watched it all the way into the corner of the net. I'll never forget the ovation. I haven't heard anything like it in my life, and I don't think I ever will again."

The power-play goal, scored at 5:38 of the third period on March 12, 1966, eluded New York Rangers goalie Cesare Maniago from about 40 feet away. The goal initiated a seven-minute standing ovation for the Golden Jet, who, since arriving in the Windy City as a swashbuckling 18-year-old in 1957, had been the catalyst for the once moribund Chicago Black Hawks regaining the hearts — and raucous vocal support — of then dwindling Chicago Stadium crowds.

After he scored the goal that put him alone among NHL shooters, Hull skated around the edge of the ice grabbing the hands of delirious fans who were leaning over the glass to share the moment they had known would come.

Like the four-minute mile — the once unthinkable barrier that now stands as a benchmark for runners looking to make the leap to elite-level competition — the 50-goal season in the NHL had become a reachable but spectacularly rare standard. Hull first hit the mark in 1961–62, a year after Geoffrion had become only the second player to reach the milestone. But Hull's repeated assault on the total (five times in 10 seasons), combined with a massive NHL expansion in 1967, helped pop the cork. In the 10 years after Hull beat Maniago for his 51st goal, there were 24 50-goal seasons recorded in the NHL. Every Original Six team outside Toronto had registered at least one 50-goal season by 1973, and even an expansion team could boast one — Philadelphia's Rick MacLeish potted an even 50 goals and 50 assists that year.

Hull's ascension to hockey royalty had been expected since he and, to a similar degree, Frank Mahovlich

arrived in the NHL as teenagers with lethal shots and speed down the wing. Mahovlich nearly beat Hull to the 50-goal mark, coming two twine busters shy of the total in 1960–61, the year before Hull would notch his first 50. Then, as Hull perfected the severely curved blade of his stick — an innovation credited to teammate Stan Mikita — and his shot became faster and harder with a less predictable flight path, Hull's name was carved among the most feared shooters of all time. His slapper was once timed at 118.3 miles per hour.

His arrival in Chicago coincided with the emergence of many young stars in the Black Hawks' system who helped the team rebuild after a stretch of 12 seasons from 1946–47 to 1957–58 with only one playoff appearance. By the summer of 1961, Hull's third season with the club, the Black Hawks were Stanley Cup champions.

With hockey alive and well in Chicago, Hull became the face of the league. He won his first Art Ross Trophy the year before the Black Hawks won the Cup, and he won back-to-back Hart Trophies in

1964–65 and 1965–66.

That 1965-66 Chicago club had the most prolific offense in the league, edging the Montreal Canadiens by a single goal. But on Hull's march to surpassing 50, Chicago went completely dry. With Hull sitting on 50 goals, the Black Hawks were shut out in the next three straight games, 5–0 by Toronto, 1–0 by Montreal and 1–0 by the same Rangers they would face three days later. The Hawks and Habs were locked in a tight battle for first place, and the 1–0 loss to Montreal and netminder Gump Worsley — who in earlier years had allowed both Gordie Howe's 600th goal and Hull's first-time 50th — was particularly concerning for Chicago.

"We're thinking about the playoffs," insisted coach Billy Reay. "There are a lot of games to play, and Bobby is going to get the record along the way."

Hull wouldn't get it until the third period of the second game of back-to-back appointments with the Rangers. When New York's future Hall of Famer Harry Howell took a penalty late in the third, anticipation began to bubble in the Madhouse on

Madison. After taking the puck from the Rangers' Reggie Fleming (a former Chicago teammate with Hull), the speedy left-winger stormed over the New York blue line and released the famous drive.

"Their defense and wingers were backing in," Hull recalled. "I stopped 10 feet inside the blue line and saw they were still backing up." And as teammate Eric Nesterenko passed in front of the net, temporarily screening Maniago, Hull let the low slapper go.

"Nesterenko lifted the blade of my stick," Maniago said matter-of-factly after the game, "and the puck went under it."

It was not the only benchmark goal Maniago surrendered in his NHL career. Geoffrion scored his 50th against him in 1961, and when Mikita registered his 500th career goal in 1977, Maniago was in net.

Perhaps because of an overfocus on Hull's breaking the record, the Black Hawks' strong season lost some steam at the end. They finished 8 points back of the Canadiens and were upset by the Red Wings in the first round of the playoffs. But Hull had a record 97 points and won the Art Ross Trophy by a whopping 19 points over Mikita. It was the last time a left-winger would lead the NHL in scoring until Alexander Ovechkin topped the column in 2008.

Hull never did win another Cup with the Hawks, but they were always in the mix, and until he made the head-turning decision to join the World Hockey Association, Chicago fans could always count on the hard-shooting star to lift them from their seats. Chicago Stadium fans had established a reputation unmatched around the league for their thunderous and raucous support.

"It was the crowd," Hull said. "When I played in that great building — Chicago Stadium — and I picked up the puck, I could feel every voice. It was like the fans were coming up the ice right behind me."

# BRETT HULL

## Controversy in Buffalo

**I**t was the second-longest game ever played in a Stanley Cup Final, and as far as hard-core Buffalo Sabres fans are concerned, it should still be going on.

In the early hours of June 20, 1999, Brett Hull's shot past a sprawling Dominik Hasek was reviewed and ruled a legal goal. It stands as the 1999 Cup winner even though Hull's skate appeared to be illegally in the goal crease.

During that 1998–99 season, a number of similar goals had been called back: a new rule stated that an attacking player couldn't stand in the goal crease unless the puck was already there. The rule was intended primarily to protect goalies from the increasing traffic in and around the blue paint.

But other than goalies, few embraced the regulation because it resulted in a number of good goals being canceled for nothing more than having a skate in the blue paint. In addition, reviewing goals delayed and defused post-goal celebrations and adversely affected the flow of the game.

Hasek's Sabres and Hull's Dallas Stars entered Game 6 at Buffalo's HSBC Arena on the evening of June 19 with the visitors holding a 3-2 lead in the series and hoping to capture the franchise's first Stanley Cup. As the Minnesota North Stars, the organization had lost in the 1981 and 1991 finals.

As the seventh seed in the Eastern Conference, the upstart Sabres were clear underdogs to the Stars, who had won the Presidents' Trophy and finished with 23 more points. Coached by Ken Hitchcock, the Stars were in win-now mode. When Hull signed a three-year contract in July 1998 after 11 seasons in St. Louis, he was regarded — correctly, as it turned out — as the final component in a Stanley Cup contender.

"It ranks number one to me," Hull recalled of the goal a few years later. "There was a boatload of people saying when I was leaving St. Louis, 'You're never going to win with Brett Hull on your team.' To go to Dallas and be the missing piece of the puzzle that's going to help them win their Cup, and then to go out and score the goal in overtime — who hasn't sat as a kid on the ice with his buddies and dreamt or pretended that's the goal they've scored?

"To do it in real life was something special."

Brett Hull moments before scoring his controversial Cup-winning goal.

It wasn't so special to hockey fanatics in Western New York, who argue to this day that the ruling on Hull's goal was inconsistent with what had been called during the regular season.

In the 55th minute of overtime, the puck came to Hull (Jere Lehtinen and Mike Modano are credited with assists) in front of Hasek, who used his stick to stop Hull's initial backhand. Hasek couldn't smother on the rebound, but he did outbattle Hull to push the puck out of the crease. The puck deflected off Hull's left skate towards his right — his stick side — as Hull's skate left the crease. As the puck landed on

Hull's stick blade in front of the crease, his left skate re-entered the painted area before he swept the puck — in unerring Hull style — through the only space Hasek had left him and into the net.

The Stars stormed onto the ice in celebration, but Buffalo coach Lindy Ruff and an arena full of his supporters were yelling, "No goal!" Meanwhile, the on-ice officials waited by the penalty box until they received the signal from the NHL's war room that the goal was legit.

"We saw that red light, and we just jumped on the ice. It was a big celebration," recalls Guy Carbon-

59

neau, who was the Stars' checking center at the time. "Once you get it to a second or third overtime, you're just happy to get that goal. There was an issue about the goal an hour later, but I don't think anyone thought about it at the time. It never came up in my mind. And then, I would say maybe an hour later, once we were in the room and drinking champagne, that's the first time we ever heard about it. But it was too late.

"It was a bad rule," Carbonneau continued. "That's why they changed it the next year. I understand the rule, but they should have written it differently. I think they realized after that that the rule didn't make sense."

The NHL's ruling was that the sequence of shot, rebound, kicked puck off the skate and second shot constituted continuous possession by Hull, which

made his skate in the crease — and the Cup-clinching goal — permissible.

"Hull had possession and control of the puck," Bryan Lewis, then the NHL's director of officiating, explained to a media horde hours after the game. "The rebound off the goalie does not change anything. It is his puck then to shoot and score, albeit a foot may or may not be in the crease prior to."

A memorandum clarifying the continuous possession concept had been circulated to NHL teams prior to the playoffs, although the media and therefore the public had not been alerted to the clarification.

"We all knew they had changed the rule," Hull recalled on a conference call just before his 2009 induction into the Hockey Hall of Fame. "But obviously, the NHL decided they weren't going to tell anybody but the teams. They changed the rule to say if you

have control in the crease, you can score the goal, and that's exactly what it was.

"But nobody knows that. You can tell people that a million times, and they just will not listen."

More might have listened had the NHL thought to inform the public about the rule clarification at the same time they informed the teams.

Hull has constantly had to defend that goal, and the always-playful wisecracker has had some fun on Twitter at the expense of Buffalo fans, who are still waiting for their first Stanley Cup championship. Ironically, Hull was a teammate when Hasek won his first Stanley Cup title, with the 2002 Detroit Red Wings.

The goal that clinched Hull's first championship was his second major moment of the 1998–99 season. On New Year's Eve he had scored his 600th goal,

which made him and Bobby Hull the first father-and-son duo to achieve that significant milestone.

But Brett's Cup winner almost wasn't. As Carbonneau remembers, Hull was sitting most of the overtime: "Brett got hurt earlier in the game — his knee, I think. And in the third overtime, Benoit Hogue broke a stick blade, or something happened to his equipment. I remember Ken Hitchcock asked Brett if he could give him just one shift, because the period was almost ending. So he jumped on the ice and …

"We still talk about it all the time. He happened to be in the right place at the right time. It's one of those stories you like to hear because Brett had an unbelievable career and had this chance to win the Cup."

It's only in Buffalo that they don't like to hear it.

# JARI KURRI

## A Hot Hand in the Playoffs

It takes a special player to stand out in his own right when playing alongside perhaps the greatest talent the game has ever seen.

The fate of Jari Kurri, the godfather of Finnish hockey excellence, could have been very different if not for the insistence of two of his countrymen, and a move by a coach looking for the right fit.

Kurri was born in Helsinki and rose through the ranks of the legendary Jokerit system as a budding professional. He was drafted 69th overall by Edmonton in 1980, but a reticent Kurri had to be convinced by Oilers Matti Hagman and Risto Siltanen — fellow Finns — to move to North America.

His plan was to stay two years, and when things started slowly in the 1980–81 season, he may have been considering cutting that short. But around Christmas, Oilers coach Glen Sather decided to put Kurri on Wayne Gretzky's wing. Together, they were magic.

Kurri had over 100 points in 1982–83, and the season after, he broke the 50-goal mark — the first of four consecutive seasons of 50 or more. He was the first Finnish player to reach both milestones.

It would be doing Kurri a disservice to suggest his

601 NHL goals were a result of being on a line with the best playmaker in NHL history. To be Gretzky's wingman, to keep up with the skill and mind of the player who was rewriting the way the game was played, Kurri needed to share Gretzky's head-space and see the game the same way as the Great One. The synergy of the duo — and Kurri's scoring exploits — allowed him to stand on his own as a premier threat. Kurri's strong defense also afforded Gretzky the offensive freedom he needed to be great.

The Oilers won the team's first Stanley Cup in 1984, and in 1984–85, Kurri had career highs of 71 goals — a single-season record by a right-winger — and 135 points, finishing second to Gretzky in the scoring race and winning the Lady Byng Trophy.

The Oilers beat the Philadelphia Flyers for their second-straight Stanley Cup that year, and Kurri had four hat tricks in the playoffs, including one four-goal game. He scored 19 goals, which tied the playoff record set by the Flyers' Reggie Leach in 1976.

The Oilers appeared to be an unstoppable dynasty in the making, but they lost in seven games in the

1986 Smythe Division final to the Calgary Flames when defensemen Steve Smith accidentally — and infamously — shot the puck into his own goal when a breakout pass hit goalie Grant Fuhr and caromed into the Oilers' net.

In 1987 the Oilers were back in the Stanley Cup, seeking redemption and their third championship in four years. It was a rematch with the Flyers, who now had Vezina Trophy winner Ron Hextall in net.

Edmonton won the first two games at home, with Kurri scoring the overtime winner in Game 2. The Oilers took a 3–0 lead in Game 3 in Philadelphia before the Flyers stormed back with five unanswered goals to win. They were the first team to come back from a 3–0 deficit to win a game in Stanley Cup Final history.

The Oilers won Game 4 to go up 3-1 in the series and had a two-goal lead in Game 5 at home, but the Flyers rallied again to win 4–3.

The Flyers weren't daunted by another two-goal deficit in Game 6, winning 3–2 to send the series back to Edmonton for Game 7. Hextall made 40 saves in the deciding game and won the Conn Smythe as playoff MVP, but the Oilers won the game 3–1 — and the series — thanks to Kurri's 15th goal of the playoffs, a wrist shot off a Gretzky pass with five minutes left in the second period, which held up as the Cup winner.

On a team with six future Hall of Famers, Kurri led the playoffs in goals each of the four years the Oilers won the Cup, from 1984 to 1988.

Kurri finished his career as the highest-scoring European-born player in NHL history, and his 106 goals and 233 points in 200 career playoff games both remain third in history, behind fellow Oilers and Hall of Famers Gretzky and Messier.

As Oilers personnel director Barry Fraser said in the midst of their glory days, "We've got some outstanding people, eh? All-Stars, right? But Kurri is by far our most complete player."

# GUY LAFLEUR

## "Too Many Men" Power-Play Goal

Ｎew Englanders simply call it "Too Many Men," usually under their breath, accompanied by a string of colorful, unprintable adjectives.

Michael Farber of *Sports Illustrated* called it "the most significant penalty in the history of major sports in North America."

Canadians remember legendary CBC announcer Danny Gallivan's call: "Lafleur, coming out rather gingerly on the right side ..." The words and images are now part of Montreal Canadiens lore.

On May 10, 1979, the Montreal Canadiens hosted the Boston Bruins in Game 7 of their Stanley Cup semifinal series. Conditions seemed to favor the Habs: the home team had won each of the first six games, and while Boston had Bobby Orr and a big, tough, skilled team, Montreal had nine future Hall of Famers in its lineup. The Canadiens were also three-time defending Stanley Cup champions, having won the last two against the Bruins.

Don Cherry, winner of the Jack Adams Award in 1976 and still some years away from becoming Canada's most famous and notorious hockey commentator, was the Bruins' coach. The image of Cherry sarcastically acknowledging the Forum faithful while standing on the boards is seen weekly during the introduction of his Coach's Corner segment on *Hockey Night in Canada*.

Many think the gesture was a response to the history-altering penalty for having too many men on the ice, but it was in fact prompted by a hooking penalty on Bruins defenseman Dick Redmond earlier in the wild third period.

According to then Bruins general manager Harry Sinden, the only sure things in life were "death, taxes and the first penalty in the Forum."

The questionable hooking call wasn't the first penalty in Game 7, and it wasn't even the most significant of the period. With the Habs trailing 3–1 after two, Montreal's Mark Napier scored before Guy Lapointe tied it on the power play while Redmond was in the penalty box.

But the Bruins shocked the Forum faithful when Rick Middleton bounced a backhander off goalie Ken Dryden from a bad angle. Less than four minutes stood between a Bruins upset and the end of a Montreal dynasty.

"We were all overhyped," remembers the Bruins' Mike Milbury. "In the emotion of the moment, we displayed a lack of awareness, a lack of restraint, a lack of discipline."

With 2:34 left to play and the Bruins clinging to a one-goal lead and Stanley Cup dreams, they were whistled for having too many men on the ice. Whether it was the handiwork of the ghosts of the Forum or of Cherry trying to keep Don Marcotte on the ice to shadow Lafleur while he double-shifted, linesman John D'Amico and referee Bob Myers had no choice. The Bruins had violated Rule 18 (now Rule 74.1), and everyone could see it.

"I can see D'Amico — hand in the air — look up with sad eyes, like, 'Sorry, Grapes, I gotta call this,'" said Cherry.

On the ensuing power play, Montreal coach Scotty Bowman put out Larry Robinson, Serge Savard, Steve Shutt, Jacques Lemaire and Guy Lafleur. All five players are now in the Hall of Fame.

Even among such stars, Lafleur's aura stood out. He was a living legend in French Canada, heir to Maurice Richard and Jean Béliveau as the king of the team, sport and province.

Béliveau retired in 1971, the same year the Canadiens secured the first overall pick from the California Golden Seals to select Lafleur, who had just led the Quebec Remparts to the Memorial Cup title.

"When I was a kid, all we saw on TV was the Canadiens, and all I wanted to be was Béliveau," said Lafleur. "We had one *bleu, blanc et rouge* Canadiens sweater, and I fought the others for the right to wear

Brian Engblom: "Guy had such a pure shot. He'd go out early for practice, and he'd take eight or 10 pucks to the top of the right circle. Then he'd start shooting. It was like a click off a golf club. Click, bang — post and in. Click, bang — crossbar and in. His sense of the net, his sense of the corners, was beyond normal human comprehension. That was a great goal because it was Flower."

Yvon Lambert scored at 9:33 of overtime to win the game and the series, and the Canadiens went on to take their fourth consecutive Stanley Cup by defeating the New York Rangers in five games. Lafleur had 10 goals and 23 points in 16 playoff games.

That was the end of an era. In the off-season, Bowman went to Buffalo, Lemaire left to play and coach in Switzerland, and Dryden and captain Yvan Cournoyer retired. The outcome of the series also helped spell the end of Cherry's time in Boston.

"Not to be disrespectful, but for a lot of people, Too Many Men was a little bit like when Kennedy was shot," says Cherry. "People come up to me all the time and tell me where they were when it happened. They tell me stuff like they were watching it with their dad in the basement, and it seems like yesterday. Bruins fans'll say, 'You don't know how I felt.' I tell 'em, 'Yes, I do.'"

The goal remains a defining moment in the NHL's most passionate rivalry and in the Hall of Fame career of its scorer. "It's who Lafleur was. It marked his greatness," said Milbury.

"What could be more appropriate?" asked Gallivan on the broadcast, after letting the mayhem in the stands and the image of a dejected Gilbert sitting on the ice speak for itself.

"Has there been a more exciting right-winger than Guy Lafleur?" wrote legendary Montreal hockey writer Red Fisher, who covered Richard and Gordie Howe. "Sure, Howe was stronger, scored more goals and lasted much longer, but was there anyone more exciting than a Lafleur, golden mane flying, skipping and dancing beyond one man and then another and then, in one motion, releasing that wonderfully accurate shot of his?

"At his best — in 961 regular-season and 124 playoff games with the Canadiens — Lafleur was not merely hockey's finest and most exciting player. He was its artist, its sculptor. With his speed and hissing shot, which produced 518 Canadiens regular-season goals, he could turn games into things of beauty."

it. I dreaded to be drafted by any other team but the Canadiens, and when they took me I was so happy."

Entering the 1978–79 season, Lafleur was the two-time reigning Hart Trophy winner, and his 52 goals and 129 points that campaign were part of a run of six straight seasons of 50 goals and 100 points — an NHL first. He was the quickest in history to 1,000 points and simply the best player on one of the best teams ever assembled, so on the Too Many Men power play, the puck was going to go through him.

"Any time you've got Lafleur in the lineup," said Robinson, "you've got a chance."

Lafleur started the play in his own end, passing the puck up to Lemaire at the Bruins blue line. Lemaire took the zone and dropped the puck back for Lafleur, who then skated "gingerly" — as Gallivan put it — down the boards, in contrast to his usual blazing speed. He retrieved Lemaire's drop pass behind the faceoff circle and hammered it past Gilbert. With 74 seconds left to play, the game was tied.

It was a "one-in-a-hundred shot," recounted Bowman.

It wasn't luck, according to Montreal defenseman

# MARIO LEMIEUX

## 5 Goals in Five Ways

**U**nlike most of Mario Lemieux's outrageously brilliant accomplishments — so immediate and so gasp inducing — this one took a little while to sink in.

And it will take a lot longer to match, although most hockey observers believe it never will be. It would take a perfect storm, including a score close enough to produce an empty-net situation, and it would take somebody as skilled at marquee production as the Magnificent One.

On December 31, 1988, playing in front of a hometown crowd of 16,025 revelers taking in a Pens game against the New Jersey Devils before ringing in the New Year, Lemieux scored 5 goals. That's a rare enough occurrence in itself, although a little more frequent for the likes of him and fellow outlier Wayne Gretzky, but Lemieux went one mammoth step further on this celebratory night.

Each goal was scored in a different manpower situation: at even strength, on a power play, short-handed, on a penalty shot and into an empty net. No player had ever scored in five different ways before the Cinco de Mario, and no player has ever done it since.

"Quite frankly, nobody was aware until the score sheet came down and you looked at it," longtime Penguins broadcaster Mike Lange recalled later. "The first thing you think is, 'Has anybody ever done this before?' The actual truth was that nobody said, 'Look, if he scores an empty-netter ...' No, it wasn't that way at all."

Lemieux scored his final goal of the record-setting game at 19:59, with goalie Chris Terreri, who had replaced starter Robert Sauvé, sitting on the New Jersey bench as the Devils tried to even the score at 7–7. There was some talk that time should already have expired, but the fifth goal counted.

By then, he had scored an even-strength goal at 4:17 of the first period followed by a shorthanded goal at 7:50, and he then completed his opening-frame natural hat trick with a power-play goal off a slap shot at 10:59. That gave him his fourth hat trick of a season that was not yet half over. All were scored against Sauvé, who allowed five goals on 10 shots. He was starting in place of regular goalie Sean Burke, who was injured.

In the middle of the second period, Terreri, re-placing the struggling Sauvé, found himself caught out of his own net with Lemieux bearing in on the only Devil in the defensive zone. In desperation, the goalie threw his stick, resulting in the penalty shot call. Of course Lemieux scored, leaving only an empty-net goal remaining in the Mission Impossible he didn't really know he was on. Some karma had to be involved as the Devils kept it a one-goal game, enabling them to pull their goalie late, but that's the kind of year it was for Lemieux.

The Mario Cycle, as it became known, is consid-ered by many to be the greatest individual scoring performance ever, especially when you consider he also assisted on each of the other three Penguins goals, giving him 100 points for the season — less than a week after Christmas.

"That was Mario's Christmas gift, a little late, to me and the fans," Penguins coach Gene Ubriaco said after the game. "I'm not going to say it was awesome — I've said that too many times before. What can I say? Someone once said we are a one-man team and certainly tonight … when he makes up his mind, no one can stop him."

Many of the game's leading players of the era acknowledge that the already-ascendant Lemieux had taken a massive step forward 16 months earlier, when he stood out among more seasoned players on Team Canada in the 1987 Canada Cup. His tourna-ment was capped by scoring the winning goal on a drop pass from Gretzky in the championship game at Copps Coliseum in Hamilton, Ontario. And that perception of greatness arrived was borne out over the next couple of seasons. He went directly from Team Canada to a 168-point regular season, up 61

Mario Lemieux hoists the Stanley Cup following the 1991 final.

points from the previous year, then had the best statistical year of his career in 1988–89, with 85 goals and 199 points.

What is stunning is that in NHL history a player has scored 8 or more points in a single game only 16 times. Lemieux accounts for three of them, all in that 1988–89 season, including one in the play-offs against cross-state rival Philadelphia. In that rampage against the Flyers, he tied the NHL records for most goals and points in a playoff game, most goals in a playoff period (4), and most assists (3) in a single postseason period. Of the nine other players who have recorded 8 or more points in a game, only Wayne Gretzky had done it more than once.

"It was a good game," he grossly understated after the historic performance. "It seems everything I did went the right way. I had the day off yesterday and that helps me, particularly at this time of the year."

According to Joe Starkey's *Tales from the Pittsburgh Penguins Locker Room*, Lemieux asked locker-room attendant Tracey Luppe, who'd been with the club for a few years but had never taped the star's sticks, if he wanted to do so that night.

"Well, he goes out and scores 5 goals in five different ways," Luppe recalled in 2004. "Needless to say, I'm still doing them today."

Lemieux lost the Hart Trophy to Gretzky that year, sparking an industry-wide debate. He had not only led the league in most scoring categories — goals, assists, points, power-play goals, shorthanded goals

and hat tricks — but he was also a plus-41 for the Penguins, a team that scored two fewer goals than it allowed. Lemieux's two linemates (Bob Errey and Rob Brown) were the only other players on the team with a plus rating.

Powered by Lemieux's 8-point nights and his 199-point regular season, the Penguins made the playoffs for the first time in seven years. They were eliminated in the second round, but Lemieux had 17 points in 11 games, establishing himself as the same undeniable force in the playoffs that he had become in the regular season.

"He did things on the ice that 95 percent of us in this league only dream of doing," said Hall of Famer Ron Francis, who joined Lemieux in Pittsburgh for his two Stanley Cups.

Seventeen years after his 5-in-five New Year's Eve, Lemieux played his last game, and, befitting of a man who had always attracted the spotlight (he scored on the first shift — and first shot — of his NHL career), he had a goal and an assist against the Flyers in a losing playoff effort. He was asked on the eve of his retirement how he would like to be remembered.

"As a winner," he said. "As someone who started with the worst team in the NHL back in 1984 and was able to win a Stanley Cup seven years later. This was a big challenge for me. To be able to do that is something I am very proud of and something I can take with me and cherish for a long, long time."

# FRANK MAHOVLICH

## Mid-Career Resurgence Fuels Unlikely Championship

For Montreal Canadiens fans, the spring of 1971 was marked by Jean Béliveau's last hurrah, Ken Dryden's astounding goaltending debut, Henri Richard's bitter public criticism of coach Al MacNeil and a dramatic postseason run. Almost always overlooked, however, is Frank Mahovlich's spectacular scoring — and timing — during that spring's playoffs.

The Big M, traded to Montreal from Detroit just three months earlier, had found comfort and inspiration playing with the Canadiens and his younger brother Peter, and he helped the Habs win what was arguably the most unexpected Cup in franchise history.

Mahovlich set a postseason scoring record with 27 points and led all playoff scorers, with 14 goals. Those goals were vitally important as the underdog Canadiens upset the heavily favored Boston Bruins — the defending Stanley Cup champions — in seven games in the quarterfinals. The Canadiens went on to defeat Minnesota in six games and then edged Chicago to become just the second team in NHL history to clinch the Cup in a Game 7 on the road.

"While Ken Dryden was getting it done defensively, Mahovlich was unstoppable on offense," Montreal's iconic hockey columnist, Red Fisher, recalled years later. "It's unlikely the Canadiens would have won the Cup without him."

In the arc of Canadiens history, Mahovlich's three years in *bleu, blanc et rouge* represent the goal-scoring bridge between Béliveau's waning years and the ascendance of Guy Lafleur. But in the spring of 1971, he was the overwhelmingly dominant offensive force.

"For the first time in his career, Frank does not have big pressure on him," Béliveau said at the time. "He always used to be a tense man. Now look at him; he is so relaxed."

The uncommonly tranquil Mahovlich did not register his first point of the playoffs until the last 80 seconds in the second game of the Boston series: he potted an insurance goal that put an exclamation point on one of the greatest single-game playoff recoveries in franchise history. The Habs, behind 5–1 in the second period, scored six unanswered goals to win the game 7–5 and tie the series.

"It was a helluva comeback," recalled Mahovlich,

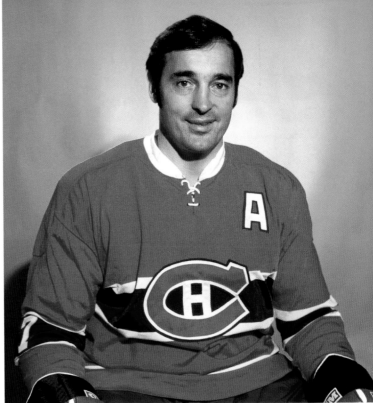

the North Stars in the semifinal Mahovlich scored his first goal of the final in a losing cause to Chicago in Game 2. He then got the tying goal and the insurance marker as Montreal closed the gap with a 4–2 victory in Game 3 and recorded a key assist as the Canadiens knotted the series in Game 4.

With Montreal needing to win after the Black Hawks had taken a 3-2 series lead in Game 5, Mahovlich was in on three Montreal goals in Game 6, almost single-handedly forcing a seventh game. He assisted on a tying goal in the first period and tied the score at 2 with a goal early in the third period, before setting up Pete Mahovlich's shorthanded game-winner in the third period. He also missed a penalty shot against Tony Esposito.

Montreal won Game 7 with a pair of goals from Henri Richard, who always said 1971 was the greatest of his 11 Cup triumphs because of the ongoing friction with coach MacNeil.

With 4 goals and 8 points against the Black Hawks, Mahovlich outscored Bobby Hull in the first final series in nine years to match the two swashbuckling left-wingers against each other. He also outshone his brother Pete, who had 5 goals and 7 points in the series.

And while Dryden won the Conn Smythe Trophy as best playoff performer, it could just as well have been Frank Mahovlich, whose acquisition from the Red Wings has been described as the best midseason pickup in league history.

whose father, Pete Sr., was in the audience to watch his sons play. "But I think the next game was the big one."

After that Game 2 insurance marker, Mahovlich scored three of the Canadiens' next four, including the winning and insurance goals as Montreal beat Boston 3–1 in Game 3.

The Habs dropped the fourth and fifth games — as expected — but Mahovlich had 2 assists in Game 6 to extend the series, scored in the first period of Game 7 to tie the score at 1 and fired an insurance marker early in the third to give him 10 points in the series.

After he contributed 9 points to the elimination of

# LANNY McDONALD

## Making His Last Goal Count

Lanny McDonald could be excused if he thought he'd never score a bigger goal than his overtime winner for the Toronto Maple Leafs in Game 7 of the 1978 quarterfinal against the New York Islanders.

Playing with a broken wrist and a broken nose, McDonald took a pass from defenseman Ian Turnbull and flung it past Islander goalie Chico Resch, giving Toronto an upset victory in the series and its first trip to the Stanley Cup semifinal, in 11 years.

Put simply, it was going to take an extraordinary moment to overshadow that feat.

That moment arrived at 4:24 in the second period of Game 6 of the 1989 Stanley Cup Final, when McDonald converted an extraordinarily accurate pass from 22-year-old Joe Nieuwendyk to put the Flames up 2–1. It would turn out to be the final goal of his career, and McDonald scored it at the Montreal Forum, the rink where he had scored his first NHL goal 16 years earlier.

Although teammate Doug Gilmour would score a third-period power-play goal that was officially the Cup winner and later add an empty-netter to seal

the Calgary Flames' 4–2 victory over the Montreal Canadiens, it was the McDonald goal that put the Flames ahead for good on their way to their only Stanley Cup title.

"It was the highlight, no question," McDonald says of the 1989 Cup win and the goal that came in the last game of his admirable career. "First of all, you always dream of scoring a goal that would help win the Stanley Cup, so in Game 6 you score the go-ahead goal. It doesn't get much better than that — especially in the Forum, against Montreal and against Patrick Roy."

McDonald, raised in Hanna, Alberta, was the team captain for that game, but he had been left out of the lineup for the series' previous three games, making the championship even sweeter.

"The Islander goal when no one gave us a chance

Lanny McDonald hoists the Stanley Cup following the 1989 final.

to win one game — let alone four — was special ... Both goals stand up, and up until then, the Islander goal was the highlight. But to help win the Stanley Cup — I'd have to say that's the best. For a guy from the West, to be [part of] the only team ever to win the Stanley Cup on Canadiens ice ... There was no way we wanted to go to Game 7 ... "

McDonald, now the chair of the Hockey Hall of Fame board of directors, wore two of hockey's most historically prestigious numbers during his career with Toronto, Colorado and Calgary. He beat the Islanders with No. 7 on his back in 1978 and was No. 9 when he and three teammates broke in on the Montreal defense in Game 6 of the '89 final.

"I had been in the penalty box," McDonald recalls. "I had missed a great opportunity then hooked Bobby Smith, trying to get the puck back. I came out of the penalty box and jumped right in on a 3-on-2. Jamie Macoun fed up to Hakan Loob, up through center. We get over the far blue line, and now it's a true 3-on-2. Loob over to Nieuwendyk, who was on the left side, and in one motion he threw it all the way across to the right side. I don't think a lot of people realize what a great pass it was. It went between Chris Chelios' skates and his stick — a very hard pass and right on the stick.

"We knew that when it went side to side, Patrick Roy goes down and tries to cover as much net as possible. And the only place was top shelf [glove side]. And when that puck went in, I was like, 'Oh my God, let's stop the game right now and get out of here.' But we had a period and a half left to play."

McDonald, who had recorded his 500th regular-season goal, 500th assist and 1,000th point earlier in the year, was the first Flame to hoist the Cup. Watching that game, his best friend and former teammate, Darryl Sittler, says he had a tear in his eye. For his part, McDonald described the victory as the "most peaceful" feeling he'd ever had in hockey.

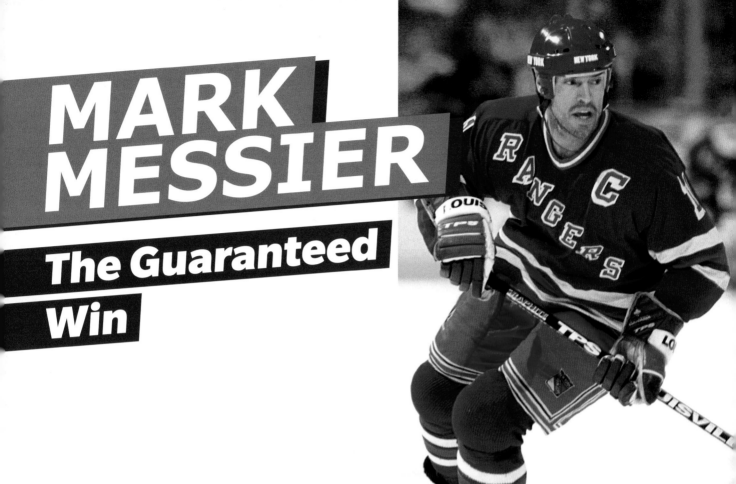

# MARK MESSIER

## The Guaranteed Win

**B**abe Ruth's called shot in 1932. Joe Namath's Super Bowl guarantee in 1969. When it comes to legendary New York sports moments, they don't get much bigger. But there's debate that the Babe didn't actually call his shot, and Namath's guarantee was hardly the boisterous proclamation historical revisionists claim. There's no debate, however, about what Mark Messier said to reporters when his New York Rangers were facing elimination in Game 6 of the Eastern Conference final against the hated New Jersey Devils.

"We're going to go in there and win Game 6."

Messier was already a star when he arrived on Broadway. He could have retired after his Edmonton days as one of the all-time greats, but he had another chapter to write.

In Edmonton, Wayne Gretzky was an artist, and Messier, the 48th overall pick in 1979, was "the Moose." He was the prototype of the ideal hockey player — equally able to bull his way through opponents, elbows and fists high, or fire the puck inside the post with his signature leg kick. Often both on the same shift.

The Oilers were swept in their first Stanley Cup Final by the New York Islanders in 1983, but a year later the script was flipped, and Edmonton ended the Islanders' run of four straight championships. With the Islanders blanketing Gretzky in the 1984 final, Messier took control of the series — and the Conn Smythe trophy — as playoff MVP. It was the first of four Cups in five years for the Oilers.

In 1989–90, as captain and undisputed leader after his running mate Gretzky had decamped for the Los Angeles Kings, Messier had his highest regular-season point total (129) and won his first Hart Trophy as league MVP. He also led the Oilers past Gretzky and the Kings in the second round of the playoffs and to the franchise's fifth Stanley Cup.

"I don't think I've ever seen any of the leaders that I've ever had do it as well as Mark did that particular year," said Oilers coach John Muckler.

But just as Gretzky ended up in a major American market, Messier was traded to New York in 1991.

According to Doug Weight, who broke into the NHL with the Messier-led Rangers in 1991 and later captained the Oilers and Islanders, "He was fierce, he

led by example [and] things weren't going to be accepted. As a team, whether you were 18 or 19 like me or you were a veteran, he was going to let you know what he expected.

"It's a tactful thing, treating people with respect, but also being able to make people accountable when you need to. It's uncomfortable at times. It's something I forced myself to do. A lot of it was him; he had an aura about him. Even when you were pissed at him, you wanted to play for him. That's a real talent, and you knew he was genuine because you had a relationship with him. I took a lot of that with me."

Messier won his second Hart Trophy in his first year in New York, and after missing the playoffs in 1992–93, the Rangers earned the Presidents' Trophy in 1993–94. But fans of the Blueshirts were keenly aware that finishing first in the regular season

guaranteed nothing, and the curse of 1940 — the last year the Rangers won the Stanley Cup — was alive and well.

The Rangers lost just one game in the first two rounds of the 1994 playoffs, but in the Eastern Conference final, the New Jersey Devils won Games 4 and 5 convincingly to take a 3-2 series lead and push the Rangers to the brink.

Unprompted, Messier guaranteed to the media the day before Game 6 that the Rangers would beat their rivals across the Hudson River and bring the series back to Manhattan.

"The questions that elicited Messier's response had little to do with a prediction. But Messier's replies were pointed and direct," said John Giannone, who was a Rangers beat writer at the time. "And they carried a distinct message from the weary leader to the embattled troops: I've put my five Stanley Cup rings,

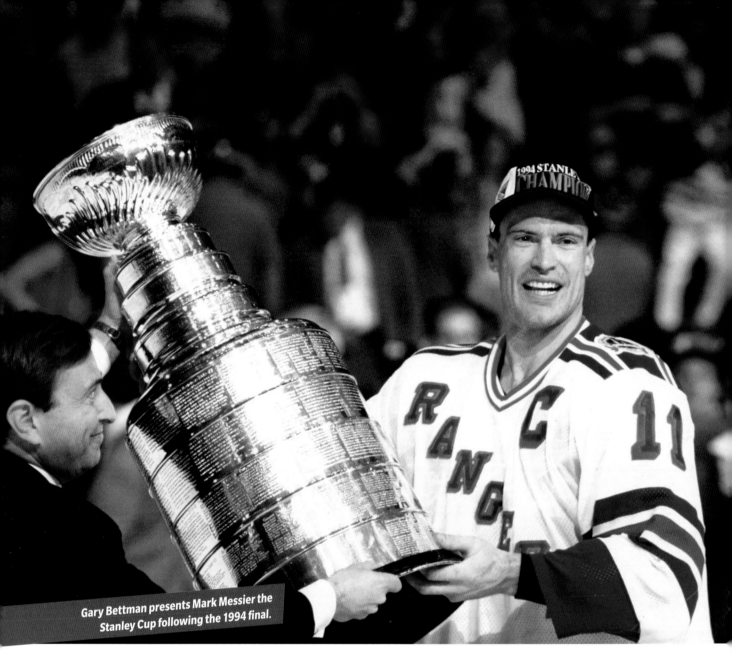

Gary Bettman presents Mark Messier the Stanley Cup following the 1994 final.

my reputation and my neck on the chopping block, boys. Now save me."

Messier recalled 20 years later: "I didn't realize, or forgot, that 14 million other New Yorkers and people around the country — and, more importantly, the New Jersey Devils — would be reading the same article. But at that point, we were so far down the tracks, it didn't really matter."

Down 2–0 late in the second period of Game 6 and facing goalie Martin Brodeur — who would set career records for wins, shutouts and playoff shutouts — it looked dire for the Rangers' title hopes and for Messier as prophet.

In an effort to spark the offense, Rangers coach "Iron" Mike Keenan decided to put slick center Alexei Kovalev on Messier's wing midway through the second period. It paid off when Messier set up Kovalev

for the Rangers' first goal late in the frame, making it 2–1 at the second intermission.

At 2:48 of the third period, Kovalev returned the favor with a pass to Messier, who scored on a backhander to tie the game. Ten minutes later, with the teams playing 4-on-4, a Kovalev slap shot bounced off Brodeur's chest and fell kindly for Messier, who bowled over a defender and slammed it into the net to give the Rangers the lead.

With Brodeur on the bench for the extra attacker and the Rangers killing a penalty, Messier intercepted a pass and sealed the win with an empty-netter from his own end.

"The stuff of legend. The called shot. The hat trick," said broadcaster Mike Emrick.

Keenan called it "one of the single most impressive performances by any hockey player in the history of

this league."

But curses aren't easily broken. It took a double-overtime winner in Game 7 for the Rangers to reach the Stanley Cup Final, where they faced the Vancouver Canucks in another thriller that went to the limit. The Canucks rallied from a 3-1 series deficit, but Messier scored the winning goal in Game 7 to clinch the Rangers' first Stanley Cup in 54 years and become the only player in NHL history to captain two different teams to the title.

Not only had he brought the Cup back to Manhattan, he mesmerized a city of endless distractions, where hockey was a niche sport. New York City Mayor Rudy Giuliani called Messier "Mr. June," and Rangers fans dubbed him "the Messiah."

Messier spent three more years in New York, including one with Gretzky, before joining the Canucks as a free agent in 1997. He returned to the Rangers in 2000 at the age of 39, and in 2004 in his 1,756th and final NHL game, he scored his 694th goal.

Messier retired with 1,887 points — the second-highest total in NHL history behind Gretzky — and only Gordie Howe played more games. He also created a legend that grows each passing year.

"So you make the guarantee, it makes headlines, and you score three goals in the third period? Seriously?" said Glenn Healy, the Rangers backup goalie on the Cup-winning team, in 2014. "How many of us have had these great plans, and they never come to fruition? Then the greatest leader in sports makes them and seals the deal with a hat trick, on his own, in the third. Never discount what Mess says. That's one thing I've learned."

# STAN MIKITA

## Slaying the Montreal Dragon

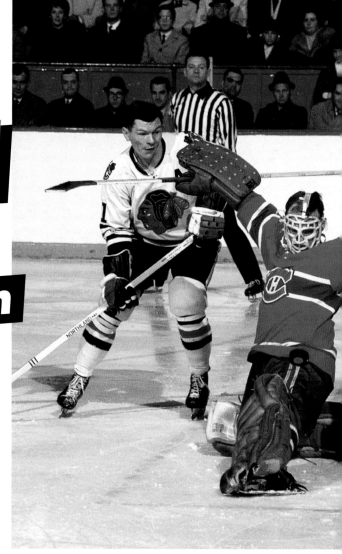

**W**hen the Chicago Black Hawks won their unlikely Stanley Cup over the Detroit Red Wings in 1961, Stan Mikita actually thought the bigger test had been Chicago's semifinal series against the dynastic Montreal Canadiens.

Mikita, just 20 and in only his second full NHL season, led the Stanley Cup playoffs with 6 goals, including the winning goal in Game 5 of the final at the raucous Chicago Stadium, which put the Black Hawks one win away from the Cup. But it was the Montreal series he savored most.

"We considered the Detroit series a bit anticlimactic," Mikita said years later. "They had some great hockey players, but we didn't think it was as big a deal as beating the Montreal Canadiens."

Montreal, who'd finished 17 points ahead of Chicago, was favored to easily advance to the final over the young Black Hawks. The Canadiens had won the last five Stanley Cups, and adding a sixth seemed likely.

"We decided, 'Let's play it together as a team and as friends and everything else,'" Mikita recalled of Chicago's late-season attitude adjustment that saw the team hit its stride as the playoffs approached.

"And you take the blame for everything that's not given to somebody. So that's what brought us together. And the attitude is what carried us through."

After splitting the first two games of the series, the best-of-seven contest swung on Murray Balfour's triple-overtime goal for Chicago in Game 3.

Montreal's Henri Richard had tied the score with only 30 seconds left in regulation time, and the Habs would have won the game if referee Dalton McArthur had not disallowed two Montreal goals in extra time. Then, midway through the third overtime period, McArthur gave Montreal's Dickie Moore a penalty. On the ensuing Chicago power play, the puck came back to the left side of the blue line, where, Mikita recalled, "I was so excited, I was off balance, and I kind of fanned on the shot, but it bounced through, and Murray Balfour put it through Jacques Plante's legs.

"That was the confidence builder we needed. We knew we could beat Montreal, but we had to show them we could do it. Surviving a marathon like that broke their spirit and bolstered ours."

The Habs won Game 4, but Chicago dominated the fifth and sixth games of the series (both 3–0 shutouts) to face the Wings in the final.

Mikita's ascendance to scoring star started during the 1960–61 season. As a rookie in 1959–60, Mikita had only 8 goals and 26 points in 67 games, and he spent far too much time in the penalty box (his 119 minutes ranked fourth in the NHL). He didn't lose any of his truculence in the Cup year (still racking up 100 minutes), but he showed the scoring touch he'd displayed in junior hockey, more than doubling his output to 53 points — including 19 goals — in 66 games.

After scoring the game-winner in Game 5 of the final against Detroit, two nights later in Game 6, he assisted on the game and Cup winner by linemate Ab McDonald to give the Black Hawks their first championship since 1938.

Mikita would go on to reach great personal heights in the years following the Hawks' 1961 Cup win. His most astounding transformation was from an ornery, aggressive player who averaged 114 penalty minutes per season (over his first six seasons) into a multiple Lady Byng Trophy–winner as the league's most gentlemanly player. In 1966–67, Mikita's eighth season, he cut his penalty minutes to 12 and was awarded the Lady Byng for the first time. Moreover, that season he also became the first player to be awarded three major trophies in a single season, snagging the Art Ross Trophy (most points) and the Hart Trophy (NHL MVP) in addition to the Lady Byng. Just to show it wasn't a fluke, he repeated the trifecta the next season.

Hawks coach Billy Reay, Chicago's bench boss from 1963–64 to 1976–77, said of Mikita's offensive awakening, "[He was] about the brightest hockey player I've ever seen. He plans every move three jumps ahead, like a good pool player. I have to say that I have never seen a better center. Maybe some could do one thing better than Stan, like skating faster or shooting harder, but none of them could do all the things that a center has to do as well as Stan does."

Mikita retired with 541 big league markers and was proof positive that a change in attitude is sometimes all it takes to make a difference.

# MIKE MODANO

## American Success Story

**I**t was a St. Patrick's Day to remember for Mike Modano.

On March 17, 2007, four days after scoring his 500th goal, Modano took a pass from defenseman Darryl Sydor at the blue line, pulled up at the left faceoff dot and fired a wrister through the legs of Nashville Predators goalie Tomas Vokoun at 10:54 of the second period. The power-play goal was the 502nd of his career, and it tied the record for U.S.-born players, previously held by Joe Mullen.

At 17:08 of the third, he slapped a one-timer from Jere Lehtinen for his second power-play goal of the game and the 503rd goal of his career. The record was his and still is.

Eight months later, on November 7, 2007, Modano scored 2 goals in the first 4:24 of a game against the San Jose Sharks to earn career points 1,232 and 1,233. He beat Sharks goalie Evgeni Nabokov on a shorthanded breakaway to break Phil Housley's record for points by an American-born player, and he did it in 1,253 regular-season games — 242 games less than Housley.

A native of Livonia, Michigan, Modano grew up a Red Wings fan, wearing the iconic No. 9 of Gordie Howe. After graduating from the Detroit Little Caesars select program, he went west to the Prince Albert (Saskatchewan) Raiders of the Western Hockey League.

While Modano was scoring 47 goals and 127 points in 65 games with the 1987–88 Raiders, the Minnesota North Stars were winning all of 12 games, earning them the right to pick Modano first overall in 1988. He was just the second American to be the top draft choice.

Known for his silky smooth skating and shot — slap, wrist or backhand — Modano became the face of the franchise as its fortunes turned around. Minnesota reached the Stanley Cup Final in 1991 but lost to Mario Lemieux and the Pittsburgh Penguins. Two years later the team moved as part of the NHL's southern expansion and became the Dallas Stars.

"The way he played the game, the way he carried himself, made him a natural role model for a number of kids," says friend and former Dallas Stars teammate Brett Hull. "I think it went from two arenas [in Dallas] when Mike came [to town] to more than 35

— and from a handful of kids playing hockey to well over 5,000. That's strictly because of Mike."

The Stars' Stanley Cup win in 1999 with an American superstar leading the way helped capture the imagination of young athletes raised on Texas football. Modano led the Stars in scoring that postseason with 23 points in 23 games, despite breaking his wrist in the second game of the final against the Buffalo Sabres.

Modano played 21 of his 22 seasons with the Minnesota/Dallas franchise and always had a flair for the dramatic — right to the end. In his final game with Dallas, he tied it up with 1:47 left in regulation and scored the deciding goal in the shoot-out, as the Stars beat the Anaheim Ducks 3–2 at the American Airlines Center.

His lone season away from the Stars was his last, which he spent in Detroit, hoping for one more shot at a Cup. But a wrist injury cut his homecoming short, and on September 23, 2011, he signed a one-day contract with the Stars and retired. He remains the career leader in both goals (561) and points (1,374)

among American players, and his 146 postseason points (58 goals and 88 assists) are also an American record.

"He probably would have had three or four hundred more points had he played in a different system, but I think Mike is going to go down as maybe the best two-way player to ever play the game," says former Dallas general manager Doug Armstrong. "He had to play [defensively] against the other teams' top players, but it was still a necessity for him to produce offense for us. Mike was a great player."

Former Stars netminder Marty Turco, who was on the ice when Modano became the top American scorer, agrees. "Mike's pure hockey ... He's about as elegant a hockey player as you'll ever see. To be on the ice when he became the all-time leading American goal-scorer, I know how special it was to him, so that was pretty cool to be part of that. But you never heard him talk about his individual stuff. Never. Maybe his long bombs on the green but never his hockey. He was too classy."

# JOE MULLEN

## America's First 500-Goal Man

**G**rowing up in Hell's Kitchen, on Manhattan's mean streets — when such a thing existed — Joe Mullen could see Madison Square Garden from his window. His dad worked at the iconic arena and brought home sticks for him and younger brother Brian to use on the asphalt of the schoolyard across the street.

The brothers learned on roller skates, using a wad of electrical tape as their puck. The cracked and craggy pavement that taught them to puckhandle was also a long way from the leafy campus of Boston College, where Mullen was offered a partial scholarship. He paid out of his own pocket as a freshman before his play convinced the school to give him a full ride the rest of the way.

At 5-foot-9, Mullen was considered undersized by NHL scouts, and he went undrafted. But after averaging a point per game at the 1979 World Hockey Championship, the St. Louis Blues signed him as a free agent. It was Blues GM Emile Francis who, during his time with the New York Rangers, had started the New York Metropolitan Junior Hockey League, which Mullen had dominated in his youth.

The Blues' offer pushed Mullen to decide between keeping his amateur status — which would allow him to play in the 1980 Olympics in Lake Placid (that team famously became the American "Miracle on Ice" squad) — or turning pro and playing in the NHL. Mullen chose pro and a paycheck to help take care of the family, because his father was ill. He made his Blues debut in the 1980 playoffs and joined the team permanently during the 1981–82 season, notching 59 points in 45 games. In 1983–84 he scored 41 goals, the first of six times he posted 40 or more.

Traded to the Calgary Flames midway through the 1985–86 season, Mullen helped the Flames reach the Stanley Cup Final that year, which they lost to the Montreal Canadiens.

Three years later he had a career-high 51 goals and 110 points, and added 16 more goals in the playoffs — the most in the NHL that year — to help the Flames avenge their loss to the Canadiens and win the 1989 Stanley Cup. Mullen capped the banner year with his second Lady Byng.

In 1990, Mullen was traded to the Pittsburgh Penguins, where, among an already potent lineup

that included Mario Lemieux, Jaromir Jagr and several other future Hall of Famers, he found a way to stand out, because he just kept scoring. In the 1991 postseason he contributed 17 points — including 8 points in the final — as the Penguins won their first Stanley Cup. The following season he had back-to-back games with 4 goals, part of a five-game, 11-goal streak. He finished the 1991–92 season with 42 goals, and Pittsburgh repeated as champions.

Already the all-time leading American scorer, on February 7, 1995, at Pittsburgh's Civic Arena, Mullen had 4 points, including an assist on a John Cullen goal 28 seconds into the second period, to become the first American-born player to register 1,000 NHL points.

After a year with the Boston Bruins, Mullen returned to Pittsburgh for the 1996–97 season, his last in the NHL. On March 14, 1997, with only 10 games left in his career and two weeks after his 40th birthday, Mullen went to the dirty area in front of the net and deflected a point shot past Colorado Avalanche goalie Patrick Roy at 16:01 of the second period.

With that marker, Mullen was the first American with 500 goals, and it was the first of a record three 500th career goals that Roy surrendered. He later allowed those of the Detroit Red Wings' Steve Yzerman and Brendan Shanahan.

Mullen was inducted into the Hall of Fame in 2000 with 502 goals and 1,063 points in 1,062 games, three Stanley Cups, two Lady Byng awards and one Lester Patrick Trophy for outstanding service to hockey in the United States.

As one of just seven players in NHL history who were 5-foot-9 or under to have 1,000 points, and as the first U.S.-born player to score 500 goals and 1,000 points, Mullen was an inspiration.

"The way people talk about Joe is pretty special. He was one of those guys who didn't have the flash, the tape on his stick was always screwed up, he kind of looked like he was fumbling the puck, but he was probably one of the smartest hockey players," says Michigan-born Doug Weight, who played with Joe's brother Brian.

"That almost sounds like a backwards compliment, but it's not. He just played the game the right way, and every year he scored goals. He just scored goals. He was a machine."

# JOE NIEUWENDYK

## A Steady Hand in Turbulent Times

The day after the Calgary Flames chose Joe Nieuwendyk in the 1985 entry draft — with a second-round pick received in a trade for local favorite Kent Nilsson — a local newspaper headline screamed, "Joe who?"

Nieuwendyk would spend his entire career giving positive answer after positive answer to that question — a career that lasted through 20 seasons, led to a place in the Hall of Fame and included three Stanley Cups with three different teams in three different decades.

A prolific scorer from the outset, he helped the Flames to the 1989 Stanley Cup, then led the Dallas Stars to the title in 1999 and got a third ring with the 2003 New Jersey Devils.

It was the middle one, with Brett Hull missing time because of an injury and Mike Modano hampered by a wrist injury, that solidified Nieuwendyk as a quietly efficient money player. A year after he tore an ACL being checked by Bryan Marchment in Game 1 of the first round of the playoffs, Nieuwendyk won the Conn Smythe Trophy as the most valuable player of the postseason. His nomination came on the strength of his playoff-leading 11 goals, along with 10 assists, and his tying of Joe Sakic's record for most game-winning goals in the playoffs, with 6.

Some goals are potted early in a game and declared the game-winner only after the final margin of victory has been determined. Few of Nieuwendyk's goals in 1999 matched that description.

When the veteran Stars swept Edmonton in the first round, giving themselves a much-needed rest, it was Nieuwendyk who scored in the 58th minute of extra play in Game 4 to eliminate the Oilers, several hours of real time after he'd opened the game's scoring.

In the next round, Nieuwendyk scored at 8:22 of overtime to give Dallas a 5–4 victory over St. Louis and a 2-0 lead in a series the Stars would eventually win in six games. In Game 2 of the Western Conference final, Nieuwendyk scored against Colorado's Patrick Roy just after the halfway point of the third period to break a 2–2 tie. The Stars went on to win in seven games and advance to the Cup Final against the younger Buffalo Sabres.

The Stars won their only Stanley Cup to date

when Brett Hull scored a still-debated goal in the third overtime of Game 6, but Nieuwendyk helped Dallas get there by scoring both goals — one of them the winner, of course — in a 2–1 victory in Game 3. He also continued to display the supremacy in the faceoff circle that had made him the NHL's leader in draws won during the regular season.

It was a remarkable spring for Nieuwendyk — and not just because of the plethora of game-winners. He had spent a grueling summer in the Dallas heat rehabbing from his ACL injury, and he had to take periodic rests during the regular season. With Hull's and Modano's nagging injuries, much of the onus of scoring fell on him.

Many Dallas fans still remember where they were when Nieuwendyk — wearing the captain's C for a week because Derian Hatcher was suspended — had Sergei Zubov's point shot bounce off him into the Edmonton net to end what was then the 12th-longest game in playoff history and launch the Stars on their Cup crusade.

"We had nothing left. They had nothing left," the soft-spoken Nieuwendyk said after the game. "Thank God it's over."

As you'd expect of a career 564-goal, 1,126-point player who honed his already-strong hand-eye coordination with years of top-level box lacrosse, Nieuwendyk had a touch around the net. He scored 51 goals in each of his rookie and sophomore seasons

and 45 or more in each of his first four seasons. He capped his second year with 10 postseason goals as the Flames won their only Cup.

But it is the Dallas championship that seems to resonate most with him.

"You hate to say one is better than the other," he said. "But there was something special about that team that you could feel in the locker room. You never think about it at the time, but that was a talented team. We were very fortunate to all be together at one time.

"I was lucky that I had a Cup in 1989, but I went 10 years without getting close again, so when I went through it in '99, I savored every moment," Nieuwendyk said. "I remember so much of that run in '99. That's when you realize how hard it is to get there. I cherished every moment of it."

So much so that he got the Cup for two days that summer, taking it to Ithaca, New York, where he had attended Cornell University, and to his hometown of Whitby, Ontario, where he and some friends put a bowl of gravy in it at a local hamburg joint and dipped their french fries.

"To me, it's the people's Cup," he said. "I just get pleasure out of watching everyone's reactions to seeing the Cup."

It was a pleasure he got to experience three times for three different teams.

# GILBERT PERREAULT

## Making Connections

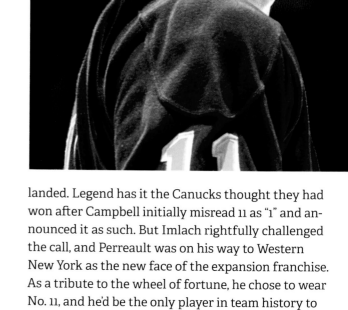

The 1970 NHL draft was set to be one to remember. With the addition of the Buffalo Sabres and Vancouver Canucks for the 1970–71 season, it was decided that the two expansion franchises would be given the first two selections in the draft. The spin of a numbered wheel would determine which club got the first overall pick — and the chance to select scoring sensation Gilbert Perreault.

A star on the Montreal Junior Canadiens (a team in the Ontario major junior circuit despite its geographic location), Perreault was Ontario league MVP in 1970, as the young Canadiens became just the third team in major junior history to win back-to-back Memorial Cups.

Perreault, from Victoriaville, Quebec, was raised on the smoothness of Montreal Canadiens stars Jean Béliveau and Dickie Moore. He emulated his heroes with skating and puckhandling skills rarely seen together.

On draft day, NHL president Clarence Campbell was given the honor of spinning the wheel. The Canucks had numbers one to 10; the Buffalo Sabres had 11 to 20. Sabres general manager Punch Imlach's lucky number was 11, and that's where the wheel

landed. Legend has it the Canucks thought they had won after Campbell initially misread 11 as "1" and announced it as such. But Imlach rightfully challenged the call, and Perreault was on his way to Western New York as the new face of the expansion franchise. As a tribute to the wheel of fortune, he chose to wear No. 11, and he'd be the only player in team history to do so.

Perreault scored his first NHL goal in the Sabres' first ever game, notching the winner in a 2–1 victory over Pittsburgh on October 10, 1970. He'd collect 511 more.

That game-winner was the first of a rookie-record 38 goals that season, which earned Perreault the Calder Trophy and kicked off one of the most successful marriages between player and franchise in NHL history.

"In my first seasons, Imlach told me to go for goals and not worry about checking," recalls Perreault of advice that would not be given in today's NHL. "That really helped me get my confidence. The first few years I was there, it was loose. I was rushing the

puck a lot. We had style."

The following year the Sabres drafted Perreault's junior teammate Richard Martin as their first pick, and after acquiring René Robert in the spring of 1972, the famed French Connection line was formed.

In 1972–73 the linemates finished the season as the Sabres' top-3 scorers and led the team to the playoffs for the first time.

The three Quebec-born players inspired the song "Look Out Here Comes the French Connection" in 1975, the year the Sabres reached the Stanley Cup Final against the Philadelphia Flyers. The series included the infamous fog game, won on a goal by Robert from Perreault in overtime. In the end the Broad Street Bullies' tough tactics nullified the Sabres' skill, and the Flyers won in six games. It was the closest Perreault got to the NHL title.

"After eight or nine years in Buffalo, I thought about asking for a trade. I wondered if a change would help my career. I was also curious to see how things were done elsewhere," says Perreault. "Even the thought of going to the Canadiens crept into my head. We had a lot of good years in Buffalo, but every hockey player wants to win the Stanley Cup.

"In the end I was glad to finish with the Sabres."

When Perreault retired in November 1986, he had 512 goals and 814 assists for 1,326 points in 1,191 regular-season games. He still holds Buffalo franchise records for goals, assists, points and games played, and he's immortalized in bronze with his French Connection linemates outside the First Niagara Center in Buffalo.

The soft-spoken star announced himself with a game-winning goal that October night in 1970, and 20 years later the Sabres retired his No. 11.

"Having a chance to play for the same team for 17 years was a highlight. In my first year I set a record in the NHL for scoring 38 goals. That was a highlight. Scoring 500 goals was a highlight. I had a lot of fun. Hockey has to be fun to be good. If the sport isn't enjoyable, then you can't be successful."

# MAURICE RICHARD

## Setting the Gold Standard

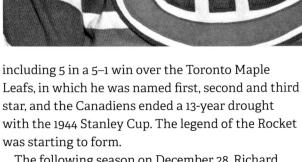

The people of Montreal have long memories, especially when it comes to their beloved Canadiens, and the city and team are intertwined as in no other place.

Maurice Richard is a pillar of the franchise's rich history, a working-class hero from the Bordeaux neighborhood in Montreal, who grew up playing in the local system. He registered under aliases so he could play on multiple teams at once, and on one he scored 133 of the team's 144 goals.

Richard joined the Canadiens in 1942 out of the Montreal Royals junior team but played only 16 games before breaking his leg. After wrist and ankle fractures in junior, which kept him from enlisting in the armed forces despite multiple attempts, some thought he might not be able to handle the physicality of the NHL.

But the league was decimated by World War II, and Richard earned a regular spot on the team. His fortitude would become a defining part of his legend.

In 1943, Richard was teamed with Toe Blake and Elmer Lach on the Punch line, and he scored 32 goals in 46 games — tops on the team and just behind the league leader. He had 12 more in nine playoff games,

including 5 in a 5–1 win over the Toronto Maple Leafs, in which he was named first, second and third star, and the Canadiens ended a 13-year drought with the 1944 Stanley Cup. The legend of the Rocket was starting to form.

The following season on December 28, Richard skipped the morning skate because he was moving his family into a new apartment. Although most of the city would've been honored to lend a hand, Richard's blue-collar roots and work ethic, along with NHL wages at the time, meant he did the job himself.

Exhausted, he asked to be excused from the game, and he was not originally in the lineup. But play he did, and two minutes into the match against the Detroit Red Wings, Richard had his 1st goal. After a respite during the first intermission, he scored 2 more goals 8 seconds apart early in the second period, before adding another goal and his 2nd assist of the night before the end of the frame. It was 7–1 after two periods, and Richard had 6 points.

Halfway through the third, Richard scored his 5th goal of the night to tie a team and NHL record

with 7 points in the game, and with just 13 seconds remaining, Lach redirected a Richard pass to make the score 9–2 and give Richard the new record of 8 points in one game. And Richard did it with a teammate's stick after breaking his own early in the game.

Richard had started slowly that season, with 9 goals in his first 28 games, but caught fire and surged past Joe Malone's NHL record of 44 goals in a single season. It was a record that had stood for 27 years.

In the second-last game of the season, referee King Clancy disallowed what would have been Richard's 50th of the season. So, in the 50th and final game of the 1944–45 season, Richard entered with 49 goals.

He stayed on 49 against the Boston Bruins for nearly the entire game. With 2:15 to play and the Bruins nursing a 2–1 lead, Richard finally broke free of the Bruins checking and beat goalie Harvey Bennett to become the first man with 50 goals in an NHL season.

Richard's feat instantly established the threshold for NHL scoring greatness and the magical number for goals in a season. It remains the gold standard for goal-scorers even now, when teams play 32 more games in a season.

According to Hall of Fame goalie Glenn Hall, who faced Richard as a member of the Red Wings and

Black Hawks: "When he came flying towards you with the puck on his stick, his eyes were all lit up, flashing and gleaming like a pinball machine. It was terrifying."

Once the puck was in the net, however, Richard was the humble kid from Bordeaux, just doing the job he was paid to do — score goals.

"While the referee waits for the clamor to subside, Richard cruises solemnly in slow circles, somewhat embarrassed by the ovation, his normally expressive dark eyes fixed on the ice," said an article in *Sports Illustrated* in 1954. "The slow circles add up to a brief moment of uncoiling, one of the few he ever allows himself. He is a terribly intense man, forever driving himself to come up to the almost impossible high standard of performance he sets."

The second 50-goal NHL season wouldn't happen for another 16 years. Former teammate Bernie Geoffrion did it in 70 games in 1961 — the year Richard was inducted into the Hall of Fame.

His record 8 points in a game stood for more than three decades, and it took 36 years until the next player had 50 goals in 50 games. Mike Bossy did it in 1980–81, the season before Wayne Gretzky scored 50 in 39 games to set the mark that still stands. Still only four players have averaged a goal per game in a

season since Richard first did it in 1944–45.

Richard's records — and there were many, including most goals in a season, in the playoffs and in a career — would be broken, but no one would represent a culture like Richard did, and no one would play the game with such flair.

"There are goals, and then there are Richard goals," said coach Irvin. "He doesn't get lucky goals. He can get to the puck and do things to it quicker than any man I've ever seen — even if he has to lug two defensemen with him. And his shots! They go in with such velocity that all of the net bulges."

*Sports Illustrated*, which rarely cast its eyes north of the border in Richard's day, called him the "Babe Ruth of hockey."

The article continues: "Because of his courage, his skill, and that magical uncultivatable quality, true magnetism, Richard has reigned in Montreal and throughout the province of Quebec as a hero whose hold on the public has no parallel in sport today, unless it be the countrywide adoration that the people of Spain have from time to time heaped on their rare master matadors."

Richard was there to say goodbye when the Forum closed in 1996, one of his last public appearances before his death in 2000. The crowd stood and gave him an 11-minute ovation before he was even introduced. He brought them to their feet as he had in the same building half a century ago. They remembered his 544 career goals and the way he played in the postseason, when the stakes were highest — the 82 goals, seven hat tricks, 18 game-winners (six of them in overtime) and the eight Stanley Cups he brought home to Montreal, including five in a row to end his career.

And they hadn't forgotten the defining moments. Nights like December 28, 1944, and the 8 points, or the series-winning goal in Game 7 against the Bruins in 1952, as blood ran down his face after he was knocked unconscious.

Or March 17, 1955, when fans revolted after NHL commissioner Clarence Campbell suspended Richard for the remainder of the season and the duration of the playoffs for punching an official. The "Richard Riot" is seen as a catalyst in the Quiet Revolution — a surging of Quebec pride and nationalism in the 1950s and 60s.

The fans stopped only when he raised his hand to quiet them, tears welling in those dark eyes as he stood on Montreal ice one last time.

# LUC ROBITAILLE

## Long-Shot Lefty Makes Good

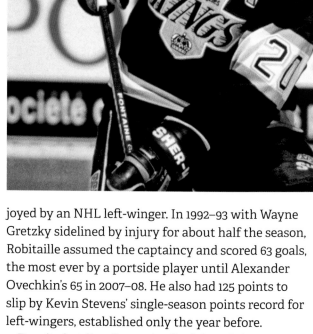

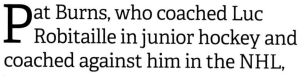

Pat Burns, who coached Luc Robitaille in junior hockey and coached against him in the NHL, had this to say about the sniper that scouts had decided was too slow to play in the big leagues: "Coaching against him in the NHL, I would always tell my teams to pay close attention to him. But while he isn't always the first to the puck, he will eventually hurt you."

The Montreal native really hurt Burns and his Toronto Maple Leafs in the spring of 1993, when he scored the tying goal to send Game 6 of the Campbell Conference final into overtime. His Los Angeles Kings won the game on Wayne Gretzky's famous (in Toronto, infamous) goal, keeping the Los Angeles Kings alive for Game 7, which they also won.

Robitaille continued scoring, adding two goals in the first game of the Stanley Cup Final. The Kings eventually lost in five games to the Montreal Canadiens, but the franchise's very first trip to the biggest series in hockey helped cement the NHL's broadening foundation on the U.S. West Coast and in the Sunbelt. Robitaille registered 9 goals and 22 points in 24 games in the Kings' run. His playoff success was an extension of the most prolific season ever en-

joyed by an NHL left-winger. In 1992–93 with Wayne Gretzky sidelined by injury for about half the season, Robitaille assumed the captaincy and scored 63 goals, the most ever by a portside player until Alexander Ovechkin's 65 in 2007–08. He also had 125 points to slip by Kevin Stevens' single-season points record for left-wingers, established only the year before.

Despite battling flu on the final day of the season, Robitaille surpassed Stevens' mark of 123 in striking style, with a goal and 3 assists in the Kings' 8–6 loss to Vancouver, their second defeat in three nights at the hands of the Canucks.

The losses to the division-winning Canucks, who finished 13 points ahead of the third-place Kings, was a brief glitch in their otherwise stellar closing weeks.

"We had a great start to the season, then we seemed to get tired and got a couple of injuries," Robitaille recalled. "But I know that in the last three weeks or four weeks of the season, we were as good as anybody in the NHL.

"Certainly, it was a lot of fun for me [to score 63], but I think it was more the success of the team that

was so much fun, because we played every game like a playoff game that whole year because we knew we were always the underdog. Until Wayne came back, we were constantly the underdog. We had a team that was really together, and we were accomplishing things that no one ever expected us to accomplish."

That could also describe Robitaille, who had only one NHL scout, the Kings' Alex Smart, take any interest in him. And even with that, Los Angeles didn't select him until the 171st spot in the 1984 draft. Three years later he was the NHL's rookie of the year with 45 goals and 84 points.

Robitaille had a very quick release. His game was about finding scoring chances, and he worked to get himself into open areas where it was easy for his centers to locate him. According to teammates, Robitaille would do anything to put the puck in the net.

"I have never been around a player who liked to score goals more than Luc," his former Kings teammate Rob Blake told the Frozen Royalty website. "He loved to score goals whether it was a game or practice. Not only did he love to score, he also knew how

to score. That is what made him one of the best."

With Gretzky out of the lineup until January 1993, Robitaille was moved up to the first line for essentially the first time in his NHL career. And it was a converted winger and future Hall of Famer in Jari Kurri who became Lucky Luc's pivot and helped him to his record-breaking goal and point totals.

"I had a new center almost every few months. Funny enough in 1992–93, they put Jari Kurri as my center, and that's the best year I ever had statistics-wise." The fact that Kurri first shot to fame as the right-winger for Wayne Gretzky was not lost on Robitaille. "It's the irony of how things go sometimes," he said.

In March 2015 the Kings commemorated Robitaille's 14 seasons in Los Angeles (over three separate terms) with a bronze statue outside the Staples Center.

"I was 13 years old in 1979, and I had a picture of Wayne Gretzky in my room," he said appreciatively at the time of the unveiling. "And I watched him on TV every time I could. Now there are statues of both of us here."

# JOE SAKIC

## Dueling Hat Tricks and Game-Winning Goals

**P**at Quinn was talking about the opening series of the 1996 Stanley Cup playoffs, but he could just as easily have been referring to that whole spring — or, for that matter, the entirety of Joe Sakic's career.

"Joe is a talented player and, over the years, has become a complete player," the consummate coach said of Burnaby Joe, who had just scored 3 goals against his Vancouver Canucks in Game 5 of the 1996 Western Conference semifinal, turning the tide towards a six-game Colorado Avalanche victory.

"I'm not too sure how we deal with him. What he does is capitalize on mistakes we've made."

In a 21-year Hall of Fame career that included a 16-season run as captain of the Avalanche and their original incarnation, the Quebec Nordiques, Sakic was always a quiet assassin, leading by example and letting his exploits speak for themselves with their loud impact.

"I'm quiet," Sakic told *Hockey Player* magazine. "I don't say too much in the dressing room. We have a lot of guys — or a few guys — that speak up in the dressing room. I'm not one of the talkers. I just try to do it by working right and working hard in practice."

And by translating that hard work in practice into mind-numbing exploits in big games.

There were many astounding moments yet to come: unselfishly handing the Stanley Cup to Raymond Bourque so he could hoist it first after the Avs' second championship, scoring the winning goal in the 2002 Olympics to break Canada's 50-year gold-medal drought, becoming the second-oldest player ever to surpass 1,000 points. But none of those exploits speak louder than Sakic's 1996 Stanley Cup campaign.

Despite the presence of franchise-changing Patrick Roy in his team's net, Sakic won the Conn Smythe Trophy after leading the Avalanche to the first championship in a major professional team sport in Denver history, putting a cherry on top of the team's debut season after it moved from Quebec City.

Sakic led the playoffs with 18 goals, just one shy of the record set by the Flyers' Reggie Leach 20 years earlier and later matched by Jari Kurri. He also added 16 assists for 34 points in just 22 games.

Sakic had 51 goals and 120 points in 1995–96, the

best regular-season production of his career, and none of those 51 goals came as part of a hat trick. But on the evening of April 25 in Denver, he scored three times, including the tying goal in the third period and the winner in overtime to match Trevor Linden's hat trick, as two quiet, let-their-game-do-the-bragging captains carried their teams in Game 5. It was the last time two men scored hat tricks in the same playoff game until Sidney Crosby and Alexander Ovechkin went equally toe to toe in 2009.

"Joe's a great player, and this doesn't surprise me," Linden said the day after the game. "We're giving him a little too much space."

With his thunderous and quick wrist shot, it could usually be said that *any* space was too much to give Sakic. There was no time in his career — even in minor and junior hockey — when he wasn't a star and when he wasn't working to get better. Cut from

Canada's World Cup team in 1991, he worked incessantly on his skating until it was no longer an issue but a strength, and on the advice of his father, he worked on his wrists and his wrist shot from the time he took up the game.

"I would shoot pucks for hours, from all kinds of different positions," Sakic recalled to the *Denver Post*. "It became something that I had to do every day, right to the end of my career. If I ever missed a day of that, I would stress out."

Instead, he stressed out goalies. Game after game.

"Joey is very hard-nosed and quick," goalie Corey Hirsch said when they were facing each other regularly in the Western Conference.

"He's got a quick release. If the puck's in the corner, he's hard after it. He doesn't let you beat him to it. When he's got the puck, it's off his stick — boom! Smart."

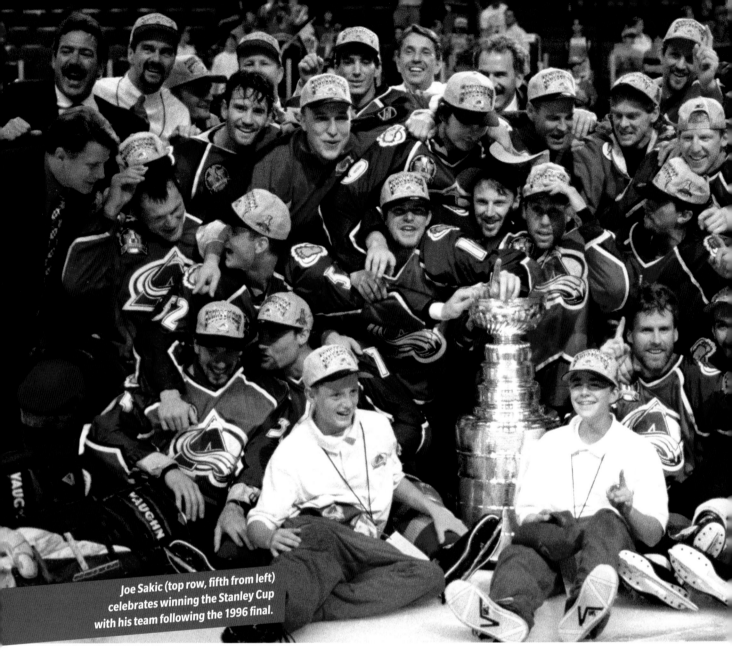

Joe Sakic (top row, fifth from left) celebrates winning the Stanley Cup with his team following the 1996 final.

Hirsch was in goal for the Canucks when Sakic and Linden traded hat tricks in Game 5.

Sakic's 1st goal was the result of a great defensive play in the offensive zone when he, seemingly innocuously, corralled with one hand a puck that was rolling out of the Vancouver zone, wheeled to the right side where he scored so many of his 51 goals that year, and let go an unexpected wrister off the wrong foot, off the post and past Hirsch.

The game-tying goal came partway through the third period from between the circles, dead in front of the net, where he had all five holes to pick from.

Then, in overtime, Sakic demonstrated just how tiny a space was, in Linden's estimation, too much to give him. Taking a nifty back pass from Sandis Ozolinsh while stationed almost against the boards at the right hash mark, he let another wrist shot go,

again off the wrong foot. Goal, Avalanche win, series momentum.

Two nights later, Sakic gave the Avalanche their first playoff series win when his snapshot off another pass from Ozolinsh with less than three minutes to go broke a 2–2 tie for his 7th goal of the series. It was his second game-winner in a row — of six he would score in the playoffs — breaking the record held by Mike Bossy, Jari Kurri, Mario Lemieux and Bobby Smith.

Sakic had 8 points in a six-game series against Chicago, then added 10 points, including two goals and an assist, in the series clincher against Detroit in a Western Conference final that set the stage for a bitter, angry rivalry that persisted for the next decade and a half.

His sixth and final game-winner of that remark-

able spring came in Game 3 of a four-game sweep of the upstart Florida Panthers, who were in just their third season in the league. He scored early in the second period to break a 2–2 tie. The Avalanche then won their first Cup in Game 4, on Uwe Krupp's famous triple-overtime goal.

Colorado became the third team to win the Stanley Cup after relocating (behind the 1989 Calgary Flames, formerly of Atlanta, and the 1995 New Jersey Devils, who had once played in Denver), but the true significance of the 1996 playoffs lay in the way they established Colorado as a solid NHL team in a viable market and heralded Sakic as one of the great playoff performers of all time.

Inside the game, Joe had always been recognized as a star, but prior to the Cup run, he had been playing in the league's smallest market, and his Nor-

diques had appeared in only 12 playoff games in his seven years there.

"The spotlight is on the playoffs, and if you haven't been there, you're not going to get noticed," Sakic said during the 1996 postseason. "This is definitely the biggest chance I'll ever get."

And he made the most of it, rising with a young team from a 12-win rookie season through a difficult move from Quebec to Denver and finally hoisting the Stanley Cup as captain, with a Conn Smythe Trophy as a bonus.

"Early on," Sakic added, "it didn't look like we were ever going to get there. Now, just to get my name on the Cup is something special. A lot of great players in this league have never won it. To be one who has, that is so special. It's something you never forget."

# BRENDAN SHANAHAN

## Meaningful Goal Caps Unforgettable Season

Brendan Shanahan never forgets the most important goals scored by other players.

As he puts it, "I remember goals, and not just mine … I have a photographic memory of a lot of people's goals — the meaningful ones at least."

Shanahan scored a pair of meaningful goals, including the Cup winner, in the fifth game of the 2002 Stanley Cup Final, which was also his last appearance in the championship series. His Detroit Red Wings defeated the Carolina Hurricanes, the direct descendants of the Hartford Whalers, the team that traded him to the Motor City just two games into the 1996–97 season.

The 2013 Hockey Hall of Fame inductee, who is now president of his hometown Toronto Maple Leafs, has no problem summoning an instant mental replay of his Stanley Cup–winning goal.

The prototypical power forward — the first NHL player to score 600 goals and incur 2,000 penalty minutes — scored the deciding goal on a power play with just under six minutes left in the second period.

"When I scored against [Arturs] Irbe, it was important, but I didn't know it was going to end up being a Stanley Cup–winning goal," Shanahan recalls. "My goal ended up being the game-winning goal, but I think the special ones are the Jason Arnott ones, the [Bob] Nystrom ones, the [Patrick] Kane ones — breaking a tie late in the game. And Darren McCarty's Stanley Cup–winning goal in '97 — my first year in Detroit — when it had been so long. I'd put all those ahead of mine."

Shanahan had been a big part of that 1997 Cup win — Detroit's first since 1955 — scoring 9 goals in the playoffs. Just the year before, he had been appointed captain of the Whalers after coming over from St. Louis in a trade for Chris Pronger. But after scoring a team-high 44 goals and 78 points in his one full season in Hartford, he asked for a trade.

It was no secret the Whalers were destined to leave Hartford, but where or when they would move remained uncertain. Shanahan says that as he entered his 10th year in the NHL, he wanted to "know where I was going to be and to have a chance to win." Whalers GM Jim Rutherford honored his request in

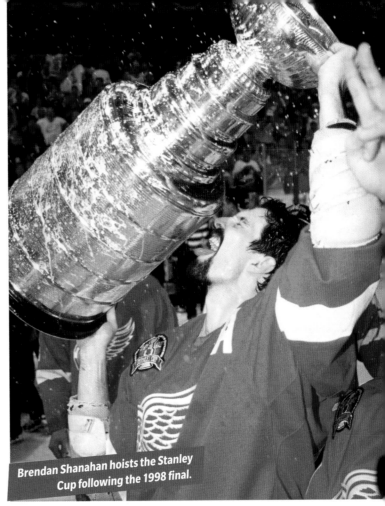

Brendan Shanahan hoists the Stanley Cup following the 1998 final.

early October 1996, sending him to Detroit for fellow power forward Keith Primeau, defenseman Paul Coffey and a first-round draft choice. Defenseman Brian Glynn also went to the Wings.

Six seasons later, by which time the Whalers had moved to North Carolina, Shanahan was facing his old club with the Cup on the line.

"Sergei [Fedorov] was down low in the right corner," Shanahan recalls of Game 5, played on June 13, 2002, "and I was on the right side farther up. Stevie [Yzerman] was down low on the other side. The puck got over to Sergei's corner, and I held up defenseman Glen Wesley to give Sergei a bit of time to get it.

"It looked like Glen Wesley and I were tied up, but when I let him go, I was open. Sergei was able to pull it from his backhand to his forehand and saucer a little pass that I was able to shoot with a short backswing — I always had a very short backswing. I one-timed it from a bad angle, but I think it caught Irbe off guard, and it didn't go in clean. I went in through what we sometimes call the eight-hole. There was actually a split second where I was taking a step in to see if I could bang in a rebound.

"It was quick. When I shot it, it looked like it was going at him, but it went through him. It went in out

of my sight. The people behind the net reacted to it ... so I had a bit of a half-delayed reaction, then realized it went in and threw my arms up."

The goal made the score 2–0 with nearly half a game to play, but two things — both of which involved Shanahan — ensured his goal would stand as the winner. Late in the second period, he took a penalty, and while he was in the box, Jeff O'Neill scored for the 'Canes to halve the deficit and make the Wings' second goal the potential winner. Then Shanahan insured the win with an empty-netter from the blue line with 45 seconds left, just as he was slammed into the boards.

"I always kid around with Jeff O'Neill: 'You and I conspired to give me the Cup-winning goal,'" Shanahan laughs.

That made Shanahan and Yzerman just the second and third players (Ken Morrow was the first, in 1980) to win an Olympic gold medal and the Stanley Cup in the same year. The win also capped a season in which the Red Wings became the first team to lose its first two playoff games and go on to hoist the Cup, and in which Shanahan scored his 500th goal (March 23, versus Colorado) and 1,000th point (January 12, against Dallas).

# MATS SUNDIN

## Working Overtime

It was only fitting that an overtime virtuoso would hit one of his highest notes in an extra period.

Mats Sundin, showing a flair for the dramatic possessed by only the game's most elite players, scored 15 regular-season overtime goals in his 18 NHL seasons. When he retired in 2009, he was tied with Patrik Elias, Jaromir Jagr and Sergei Fedorov for the all-time lead. (As of 2015–16 he remained tied with Fedorov for fourth.)

But no one else — not even the ageless wonder who is Jagr — has ever hit the 500-goal plateau after regulation time has expired.

Sundin entered the Toronto Maple Leafs' sixth game of the 2006–07 season with 497 goals and exited it with an even 500, scoring the landmark goal 50 seconds into overtime with a screaming, slightly screened slap shot from just inside the blue line that evaded Miikka Kiprusoff of the Calgary Flames.

Sundin's marker not only gave the Maple Leafs a 5–4 victory over the Flames but also completed an impressive hat trick for the Toronto captain, who was accorded a lengthy standing ovation and was named as the first, second and third stars of the game. Sundin's 1st goal of the night came on a Leafs power play, goal number 499 was at even strength and the overtime winner came with Darcy Tucker in the penalty box. The 1st and 3rd goals were from the left side of the ice; the 2nd, from the right. But all 3 were delivered with prototypical Sundin laser-beam accuracy.

Only one other player, Gordie Howe, had ever hit the 500 mark with a shorthanded goal, and Sundin is one of just seven players — all of them Hockey Hall of Fame inductees — who registered 3 goals in a game to reach 500. The other six are Jean Béliveau, Wayne Gretzky, Mario Lemieux, Mark Messier, Brett Hull and Jagr.

With his younger brother, Per, among the fans roaring their unfettered appreciation, Sundin became the first Swedish-born-and-trained player to score his 500th goal. After he scored he was mobbed

by his teammates, who tapped their sticks on the ice in his honor as they left the ice.

"It was a very special moment for a lot of guys on the team," said Tucker, who had scored earlier in the game (on a Sundin assist). "It's only fitting that he scored that huge, big goal in overtime because he's done it so many times before for us. It was nice to see the ovation from the crowd and all the guys sitting around waiting at the end of the ice.

"Even when he came in after doing his interviews, the guys gave him a good cheer in the dressing room. It was great, great to see."

Sundin, like many Hockey Hall of Famers as they approach a major signpost in their careers, was glad he could erase the distraction of number 500 early in the season.

"Certainly, I'm proud of the accomplishment, and it makes it special the way it happened — to get the win in overtime too," he said right after the game. "I'll remember it all my life.

"More than anything, it's nice to get it over with.

"I didn't want to go 15 or 20 games into the season and still be looking for it."

The goal came in Sundin's 10th year as captain

and his second-last as a Maple Leaf — the last leg of his time in Toronto unfortunately coinciding with a franchise downturn and a fan base that had become bitter and disillusioned. Sundin, however, with his determined and often-dominant game presence, as well as his poise and class both on and off the ice, usually gave fans hope. Though the Toronto faithful were slow to warm to the talented Swede after his arrival via a trade that sent fan favorite Wendel Clark the other way, by the time of his 500th goal, they had long since realized they were watching one of the greatest Maple Leafs of all time.

"We have the best fans. The team hasn't won a championship since 1967. They don't want anything else than for us to do well," Sundin said after the game. "I realized the applause and the people standing and staying in the rink for me — it was appreciation of that on my part. That just doesn't happen very often. I've been here for many years, and it was a special moment for me.

"It was very emotional. I'm obviously very proud, and I'm very humbled by the reception that I got. It was awesome."

# BRYAN TROTTIER

## From Personal Best to Team Success

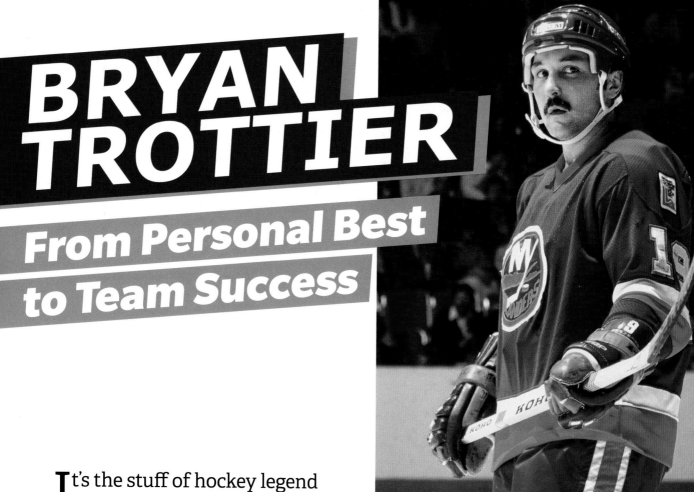

It's the stuff of hockey legend and Canadian heritage moments: a young boy hones his skills on frozen Frenchman Creek in Val Marie, Saskatchewan, and grows up to set records and lift Stanley Cups in the bright lights of New York.

"There was a beaver dam next to our house," recalls Bryan Trottier of his childhood just north of the Montana border. "Dad figured it out — chopped that beaver dam and it was like a Zamboni. We'd have fresh ice in the morning. We were spoiled rotten; we didn't know what it was like not to have good ice all winter long."

Trottier was a gentle soul, but in a more violent era of hockey, making hard fists of soft hands was considered a necessary part of the game. Dave "Tiger" Williams — who became the NHL's all-time leader in penalty minutes — was a teammate with Trottier on the Swift Current Broncos of the Western Hockey League, and he taught the talented center to fight and to survive. That apprenticeship added the grit and dogged defense to Trottier's game that would be his signature, even as he lit up NHL scoreboards.

Drafted by the New York Islanders 22nd overall in 1974 at the age of 17, Trottier joined the team in 1975 and won the Calder Trophy as Rookie of the Year after setting a then rookie record with 95 points.

Two days before Christmas 1978, Trottier set another record, which still stands.

The Islanders' hated New York rival, the Rangers, were visiting Nassau Coliseum, but vacation might've been on everyone's minds in the pedestrian first period. Trottier opened the scoring, and the game was tied 1–1 after one. Nothing suggested history was about to be made.

At 1:08 of the second period, the Rangers' Ron Duguay took a penalty, and just three seconds into the power play, Trottier set up Mike Bossy for a goal. Less than three minutes later, Trottier scored his 2nd of the night, followed even more quickly with an assist on a Garry Howatt goal. With only 5:08 gone, he had 3 points on 3 Islander goals in the period.

Trottier then assisted on Bossy's 2nd goal of the night at 11:21 and scored twice himself in the final 90 seconds of the period. The Islanders went into the second intermission with an 7–2 lead thanks to Trottier's record–setting second period of 3 goals and

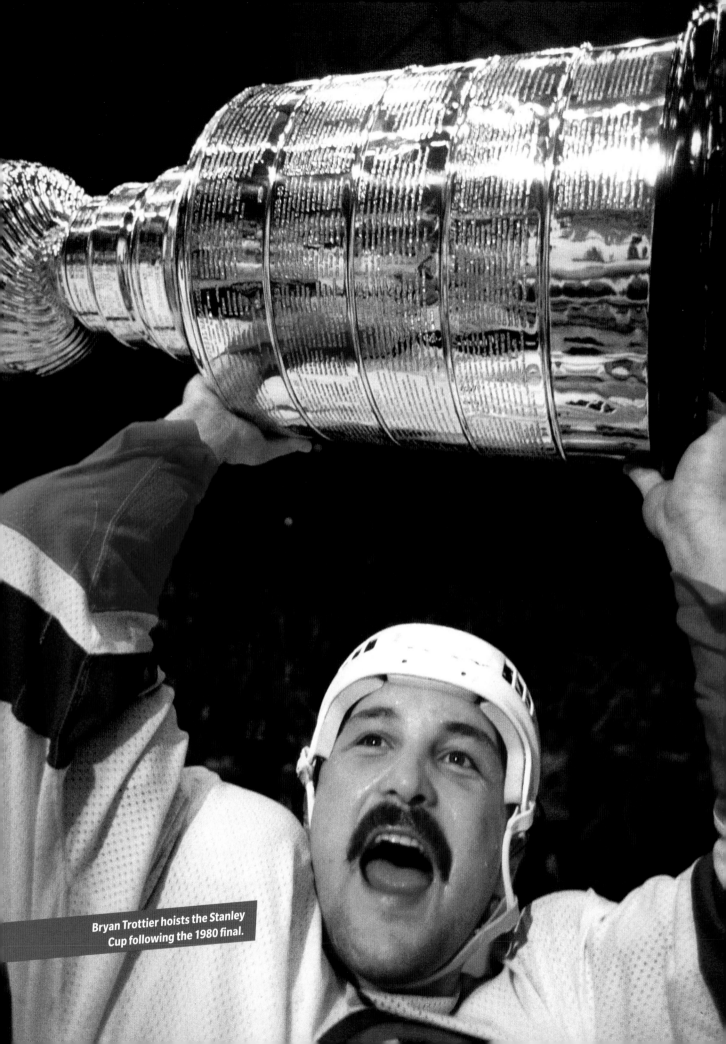

Bryan Trottier hoists the Stanley Cup following the 1980 final.

3 assists for 6 points.

Trottier added his 5th goal and 8th point in the third as the Islanders finished what started as a snoozer with a dominant 9–4 win. The victory pushed their record to 21-4-7 and extended their undefeated streak at home to 16 games (12-0-4).

To this day there have been only 16 eight-point games in NHL history (accomplished by only 13 players). However, just two players since World War II — and eight in history — have scored more goals in a game than Trottier's 5.

In the season that would see the last of the

Montreal Canadiens' four straight Stanley Cups, this regular season game signaled a changing of the guard. Mike Bossy would go on to set an Islanders record with 69 goals, most of which were assisted by Trottier, who set his own high-water mark in points, with 134 (47 goals, 87 assists). Those totals earned Trottier both the Art Ross Trophy as the league's leading scorer and the Hart Trophy as NHL MVP.

The Islanders were the top seed in the playoffs in 1979 but lost in six games to the Rangers in the semifinal. It was the last time they'd lose a playoff round for quite some time. In 1980 the Islanders won

the first of four straight Stanley Cups, and Trottier took home the Conn Smythe Trophy as playoff MVP. With a chance to win a record-tying fifth straight championship in 1984, the Islanders lost in the final to the Edmonton Oilers, the NHL's new superpower led by Wayne Gretzky.

Trottier and Gretzky were two of the best players in the game in the early 1980s, but Islanders Hall of Fame coach Al Arbour said he wouldn't have traded Trottier for Gretzky, who was rewriting the record books but never had a 6-point period.

While Arbour might've had a New York bias, journalist Stan Fischler, who's covered the game since 1954, maintained that 19 was better than 99: "Trottier has ripened into the most effective total forward since Gordie Howe."

Just as age eventually caught up with Howe, Trottier's scoring pace slowed, and he was bought out by the Islanders in 1990 after 15 years with the team. Offered a front office job, the gritty center felt he had more hockey in him, and he signed with the ascending Pittsburgh Penguins.

Trottier learned to be a professional as a callow rookie with the Islanders by watching and learning from teammates and leaders Denis Potvin and Clark Gillies. His arrival in Pittsburgh was primarily to provide the ultra-talented but young Penguins — a club that included Mario Lemieux and Jaromir Jagr — with mentoring of their own. It was a winning combination: Trottier won two more Cups with the Penguins in 1991 and 1992 before retiring. Restless without the game, he returned for half the 1993–94 season before he called it a career.

In 1,279 NHL games, Trottier had 524 goals, including 68 game-winners, and 1,425 points. He had more than 100 points in six seasons and finished his career with a plus/minus record of plus-470. He also played in eight All-Star games and two Canada Cups, once for Canada and once for the U.S. As a North American Indian, he holds dual citizenship.

"I'm very proud of my heritage," says Trottier. "My mom's Irish, my dad's Cree-Métis-French. My bloodlines are strong. There's some bullheadedness and determination built into the bloodlines, and I love it. I love my parents for it; I'm proud of it — proud of my Canadian roots, but I'm North American."

Trottier was inducted into the Hall of Fame in 1997 and was the inspiration for the next generation of complete players with 19 on their jerseys — from Steve Yzerman to Joe Sakic to Shane Doan — who could score but weren't afraid to do the dirty work that's crucial for success in the NHL.

In "Letter to My Younger Self" in the *Players' Tribune*, Trottier wrote, "It's never going to be pretty. It's never going to happen the way you plan it. Sometimes you just have to go out to the beaver dam with a machete and start chopping wood."

# STEVE YZERMAN

## Fan-Favorite OT Winner Ushers in New Era for Detroit

**S**teve Yzerman not only capped one of the greatest playoff games in NHL history but also helped usher in the nickname that has become as synonymous with Detroit as is the Motor City: Hockeytown, U.S.A.

His goal in the second overtime period of Game 7 of the Western Conference semifinal in 1996 gave his Detroit Red Wings a 1–0 victory — and the series — over the St. Louis Blues, who had finished 51 points behind Detroit in the regular season. Had the Wings lost, their reputation as postseason underachievers would have grown exponentially. The franchise hadn't won a Stanley Cup championship since 1955 and had been swept by the New Jersey Devils in the previous spring's final.

Although the Red Wings reignited their fans' passion by winning back-to-back elimination games after dropping three consecutive one-goal decisions to the underdog Blues, they would not win the Cup in 1996 either. They went on to lose the Western Conference final to Patrick Roy — against whom Yzerman had scored his 500th goal in January — and the eventual Cup champions, the Colorado Avalanche.

The following year the Hockeytown logo made its debut in the faceoff circle at Joe Louis Arena's center ice, and the Detroit Red Wings won three of the next six Cups, in 1997, 1998 and 2002.

By the time he scored the goal that broke a scoreless tie in the second minute of the second overtime of Game 7, Yzerman had evolved from the 50-plus goal-scorer of the late 1980s into a complete two-way player and a team captain. And in Game 6 of the series, à la Mark Messier, he had predicted his team would force a seventh match. They won, 4–2.

"We never sat back and said, 'My God, what if?'" Yzerman said. "It really was a different atmosphere. There was a lot of excitement, a lot of energy. People were really positive. We proved to ourselves how to approach tough games and tough situations. If anything, our attitude got better, our will got stronger and our confidence grew."

The Blues were loaded with talented veteran players, many of whom had made their reputations elsewhere. Throughout most of Game 7, Yzerman was matched against Wayne Gretzky's line.

St. Louis dominated the first overtime period, but

Steve Yzerman hoists the Stanley Cup following the 1998 final.

14 seconds into the second extra frame, Jon Casey, replacing the injured Grant Fuhr, had to make a brilliant save against Sergei Fedorov. A minute later Slava Fetisov coolly retrieved the puck in his own zone and got it to defenseman Vladimir Konstantinov, who wobbled a poor pass over the blue line that Gretzky nearly intercepted on the left side of the ice.

But the puck bounced off Gretzky's stick and then his skate and caromed to Yzerman, who angled to the right and unleashed a slap shot from just inside the blue line that caught Casey by surprise and turned the relatively quiet Joe into a screaming madhouse. Many Wings fans still call it their favorite goal of all time.

"I remember thinking in the first overtime, 'I'm just going to start shooting the puck from wherever. I'm tired and they're not calling penalties,'" Yzerman would later explain of his eighth shot of the game, 8th goal of the playoffs and 11th point of the series.

"The defensemen were just wrapping us up. I wasn't getting a whole lot done. So I picked the puck up in the neutral zone — I think Murray Baron was the defenseman — and I thought, 'Just shoot it and try to get it past his feet and not hit him.' Sure enough, I found a clear path and it found the top corner. It was kind of a lucky shot because I was just trying not to get it blocked. That was my only playoff overtime goal."

In more than one fan poll, Yzerman's series winner has ranked among the top-10 moments in Stanley Cup history. It broke more than 81 minutes of scoreless hockey in which both Casey and Detroit goalie Chris Osgood had been flawless. It was the second 1–0 game in the series: Gretzky had scored the only goal of Game 4 to tie the semifinal at two games apiece.

"I couldn't believe it went in," Yzerman said amid the Detroit delirium. "I don't score a whole lot of goals from out there. To score a goal in overtime, particularly in Game 7, is a tremendous thrill. Every player dreams of that."

# GAME-BREAKING GOALS

Bobby Orr

## April 21, 1951

## The Last Goal
## He Ever Scored

# BILL BARILKO

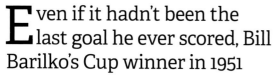

E ven if it hadn't been the last goal he ever scored, Bill Barilko's Cup winner in 1951 would have stood apart in Toronto hockey history. But when the 24-year-old defenseman went missing a few months later, his story transcended hockey and became part of modern Canadian pop culture.

When Canadian rock icons the Tragically Hip released "50 Mission Cap" in 1992, the song refocused public attention on what many Toronto fans had long regarded as the most important — certainly the most dramatic — goal in Maple Leafs history.

The wildly popular song eloquently and succinctly recounts the story of Barilko, who scored the game-winning goal at 2:53 of overtime to give the Leafs the 1951 championship over the Montreal Canadiens, in five games. Thirteen weeks later, Barilko and his friend Henry Hudson set off in Hudson's single-engine Fairchild 24 floatplane for their last fishing trip of the summer. On the return flight from James Bay to their hometown of Timmins, Ontario, the plane disappeared.

The plane and the skeletons of Barilko and Hudson buckled into their seats were not discovered until June 7, 1962, just seven weeks after the Leafs

had won their first Stanley Cup since Barilko's goal.

Fans were shocked by the disappearance of the rugged Bashin' Bill, who had offensive skill — he had scored 2 earlier goals in the playoffs — but was far better known for his bone-rattling bodychecks and superb shot blocking. His teammates, unable to accept that Barilko would likely never return, left his equipment untouched in his dressing-room stall when training camp opened in the early fall. And it wasn't until five years later that Leafs management asked the NHL to move Barilko's name to the voluntary retirement list. Barilko's No. 5, which he wore only that season (he had been given No. 19 and No. 21 before that), is one of only two numbers the Maple Leafs have ever retired.

The search for the plane had been the most costly air manhunt to that point in Canadian history, and because there had been no trace of the crash, all kinds of rumors surfaced, including one that had Barilko defecting to Russia to teach hockey.

The 1951 Cup was the only one of Toronto's 13 championships to be clinched in overtime, and Bari-

Bill Barilko scores his dramatic Cup-winning goal in 1951.

lko's goal capped the only Stanley Cup Final in which every game went into extra time. It also gave the Leafs their fourth title in five years, making them, if not arguably the first dynasty in NHL history, certainly the first dynasty in Maple Leafs history.

The 1950–51 season was just Barilko's fifth year in the NHL, and his Leafs won the Cup in four of them. But he had been warned by rookie coach Joe Primeau that he was becoming too attracted to offense, sometimes straying from the team's defense-first mantra. Accordingly, in overtime Barilko had remained just outside the blue line until the Leafs' forward line of Howie Meeker, Cal Gardner and Harry Watson got the puck deep. Meeker, battling big Tom Johnson behind the net, got the puck out to Watson, who swiped at it. The puck caromed, probably off Montreal captain Butch Bouchard's skate, into the right faceoff circle as goalie Gerry McNeil, likely anticipating Watson's shot, fell backwards to his left.

Seizing the moment, Barilko rushed forward, met the puck near the top of the circle and, possibly clipping Gardner's skate, left his feet as he let go a semi–slap shot that beat McNeil high on his right side before he could regain position. Had he missed the net, Barilko would have been horribly out of position, and Rocket Richard's line would have had a chance for an odd-man rush towards the Leafs net.

But he didn't miss.

"There have been a lot of great overtime goals in the history of the NHL, but to me Barilko's was one of the best," Watson said. "Barilko's goal was a perfect ending to a tremendous series."

Hockey Hall of Famer Max Bentley, who had set up the game's tying goal with just 42 seconds left in the third period and Turk Broda out of the net, said Barilko was fearless and, had he lived, would have been one of the greatest Leafs ever. Broda himself called Barilko the best defenseman he ever played behind.

Toronto struggled for more than a year to find a suitable replacement for Barilko on the blue line until they finally settled on Tim Horton. Fittingly, when the Maple Leafs finally snapped their 11-year Stanley Cup drought shortly before Barilko's body was found, Horton was their leading playoff scorer.

## Gladiators on Ice

# THE ROCKET & SUGAR JIM

The photograph is among the most striking images from the NHL's gladiatorial early days.

On one side stands Maurice "Rocket" Richard, one of the league's first real superstars, a cultural icon and francophone hero. On the other is "Sugar" Jim Henry, a journeyman goalie whose career was almost cut short by a freak accident.

Sugar Jim got his nickname because of his fondness for brown sugar as a youngster in Winnipeg. Signed by the New York Rangers in 1941, he led the NHL with 29 wins in his first season in the Big Apple before enlisting in the Canadian navy for World War II.

Henry spent the war in Canada and returned to the Rangers in 1945, as half of the first goalie tandem in the NHL. He was later traded to Chicago and then Detroit, bouncing around the minors with both teams before landing in Boston in 1951.

Henry and his old Rangers goalie partner, Chuck Rayner, had opened a hunting and fishing lodge in Kenora, Ontario, and a fire in the shed that summer burned Henry badly. Doctors told him he'd never play hockey again, but he reported for training camp and played 210 games in a row for the Bruins.

Rocket Richard was the first player to score 50 goals in a season, doing it in 50 games in 1944–45, and he won the Hart Trophy as the NHL's most valuable player in 1947. He had an iron will and eyes that bore holes in opponents, but he'd missed 22 games of the 1951–52 season, and a groin injury almost kept him out of the playoffs completely.

In the 1952 Stanley Cup semifinal, the Bruins ran into Richard and the heavily favored Montreal Canadiens. It was a series that helped lay the foundation for the animosity between the clubs that still exists today.

Henry shut out the Canadiens in Montreal in Game 5, and the Bruins took a 3-2 series lead. Boston held a 2–1 lead in the third period of Game 6 when Henry took a Doug Harvey shot to the face that broke his nose and delayed the game for 17 minutes. When play resumed, Richard took advantage of Henry's blurred vision and beat him from the outside to tie the game. The Canadiens went on to win in double overtime.

Richard had suffered a knee injury in Game 6, and

The Rocket and Sugar Jim shake hands following their 1952 playoff game.

in the seventh game he was blindsided by defenseman Leo Labine. His head hit the knee of a Bruin before slamming into the ice.

Richard lost consciousness on the ice and again while having his forehead stitched in the dressing room. Today, he would be sent to the quiet room and removed from the game with an "upper body injury." In 1952 he returned to the ice with four minutes left in the game, covered in blood and unable to read the scoreboard.

On the next shift, Richard took the puck on a rush and turned the corner on the defense, holding them off as he bulled his way to the net. He faked a shot before sliding the puck past Henry for the series-winning goal with 3:14 left on the clock. He later said he did it all himself because he couldn't tell which players were on his team, in the Canadiens' white uniforms, and which were in Boston's black sweaters.

"My legs were all right, but I was dizzy," said Richard. "I heard the crowd yell, and by that time I was too dizzy to see."

Richard died in 2000; Henry, four years later. But together they're frozen in time in black and white, at the height of their powers and nearly battered into submission. Richard has blood running down his face from under the bandage on his left brow; Henry's eyes are still black and swollen from the broken nose, and he's slightly bowed as they shake hands on that April night in 1952.

"I felt bad of course because he had just eliminated us from the playoffs, but I had to congratulate the Rocket because it was one of the greatest goals I had ever seen, and it was no shame being beat by such a player," Henry said years later. "Rocket Richard filled the stadiums wherever he went in those days, with the fans coming out to either boo or cheer him."

# Cup Winner Takes Flight

# BOBBY ORR

**Bobby Orr** recalls in his book *Orr: My Story* that, at one of the many events he has attended with Hall of Fame goaltender Glenn Hall, somebody mentioned — for the umpteenth time — the goal that froze them together forever in hockey history.

"He looked over at me and, shaking his head in mock disgust, asked, 'Bobby, is that the *only* goal you ever scored in the NHL?"

The answer to that question would be a resounding no. Orr revolutionized the way defense — if not hockey itself — is played. He retired with 270 goals in just 657 regular-season games — a rate of just under 34 goals over an 82-game schedule, numbers unthinkable for a defenseman. But his 1970 Stanley Cup winner was certainly the most important, significant and symbolic goal he ever scored, and it's the goal still remembered many generations later.

The memory would have lasted anyway, but Ray Lussier, the talented photographer for the *Boston Record American*, made sure of it. When the fourth game of the 1970 Stanley Cup Final at the old Boston Garden entered overtime, he found a spot along the boards in the St. Louis Blues' end of the ice that had been temporarily vacated by another photographer.

*Bobby Orr moments after scoring his famous Cup-winning goal in 1970.*

Just 40 seconds into overtime — and just before the other photographer returned — Lussier snapped the most famous shot in hockey history.

The photo catches Bobby Orr sailing jubilantly through the air — parallel to the ice — after being tripped by Noel Picard, the puck already having bounced back out of the net.

It's a complete storytelling shot. But it can't tell the whole tale of a goal that speaks volumes of history at once.

The goal that gave the Bruins a four-game sweep over the Blues was the final jewel in Orr's coronation crown as the greatest defenseman — and arguably greatest player — of all time. It gave the Bruins their first Stanley Cup in 29 years and completed the transformation of a sad-sack franchise into a model one that began with the arrival of Orr in 1966 and Phil Esposito in 1967. And with Derek Sanderson passing the puck to Orr, who had first passed it to Sanderson, the goal encapsulated the two major elements of the Bruins' spectacular revival: Boston's offensive power, evident in Orr's skill, speed and creativity; and the Big Bad Bruins' swaggering free spirit and physical aggressiveness, displayed by the cocky Sanderson.

"What made that team so special was that we had grown together since 1967," said Sanderson. "We had so much fun on that team. And as hard as we played on the ice, we played just as hard off it."

It was clear the Bruins were going to win their first Stanley Cup since the Second World War (when GM Milt Schmidt was an active player) after they dominated the first three games of the series. An early omen was a Fred Stanfield slap shot to Jacques Plante's face mask that knocked Hall's future Hockey Hall of Fame confrere out of Game 1. But the Blues had made it tough for Boston to close, leading late in the third period before Boston veteran Johnny Bucyk sent Game 4 into overtime.

Bucyk, who had been through many of the worst Bruins times, was thankful for the Orr goal, which finally ended the Hub's hockey pain.

"Everything I had ever hoped for in a hockey game came true in that 40 seconds of overtime," a relieved Bucyk said right after the most memorable goal in Boston history.

The goal capped an incredible regular season and playoff run for the Bruins and for Orr in particular.

Boston had trailed the New York Rangers in the East Division standings for most of the year, finally catching them in early March and then beating them in six games in the Stanley Cup quarterfinals. Their 81 power-play goals smashed the previous record, held by Bobby Hull's Black Hawks, by a whopping 13 percent.

That season, Orr broke records for goals (33) and points (120) by a defenseman, was the first blue-liner to win a scoring championship and became just the fourth player at any position to register 100 points. He was also the NHL's first-ever winner of four major trophies: as well as the Art Ross Trophy, he won the Hart as the most valuable player in the regular season, the Norris as top defenseman and the Conn Smythe as most valuable player in the playoffs.

In typical self-effacing fashion, the man who beat out Bob Cousy, Bill Russell, Ted Williams and Carl Yastrzemski in a poll to determine the best athlete in Boston history said he got "a little lucky" with the goal that established the Bruins of his era as one of the most prolific teams in NHL history.

"The puck was coming up the boards, and if it had got by me, it might have been a 2-on-1 against us, but it hit me," he said later. "I did see Derek and threw the puck back to him, and I went to the net. That's the way I played, and Derek gave me a great pass right on the stick. As I started to move across, Glenn Hall had to move with me, and it's pretty difficult to move across and keep your legs closed. I was just trying to put the puck on net, and I did. Noel Picard

was lifting me, but I was also jumping at the same time because I did see the puck go in. It was in overtime, so I knew it was over.

"I was flying through the air. I thought I was going to leave the rink. When the puck hit behind Hall, we'd won the Stanley Cup.

"The photographer, I mean, he got it."

For those interested in more esoteric symbolism than the end of a Cup drought and the anointing of the game's new messiah, Lussier's picture also honors the power of four. Four was of course Orr's number, and it was already rivaling the traditional No. 9 as the digit of choice for thousands of young hockey players. The Cup winner was the fourth goal in the fourth period of the fourth game of the final. And Orr was tripped by Picard, who wore ... No. 4. Orr's aura was so strong that years later Larry Bird,

another Boston Garden icon, would look up at Orr's jersey — raised to the rafters on January 4, 1979, after an 11-minute standing ovation — while the national anthem was played to gain inspiration for that night's Celtics game.

"Was it my most exciting moment as a player?" Orr asked rhetorically of the Cup winner many years later. "Well, it wasn't just the goal. My dream growing up, like most Canadians playing hockey, was to be on a Stanley Cup team. So to be on a Stanley Cup team was pretty special, pretty special."

Not just for him but for every hockey fan, including those who weren't even born when the puck slipped under Glenn Hall.

# Historic Goal Restores Canada's Pride

# PAUL HENDERSON

It is the touchstone for at least a couple of generations of Canadians. Everyone alive on the afternoon of September 28, 1972, knows exactly where they were and who they were with.

It was already late evening at Moscow's Luzhniki arena when Paul Henderson beat Vladislav Tretiak with the shot that rescued Canadian hockey pride from mortal danger, decided a minor skirmish of the Cold War and elevated "Henderson has scored for Canada" past "He shoots, he scores" as Foster Hewitt's most famous call.

When Henderson swept a rebound past Tretiak for his third straight game-winning goal in Moscow, giving Team Canada a four-games-to-three (with one tie) decision over the Soviet Union's Big Red Machine in the revolutionary Summit Series, the moment transcended the goal itself.

As Canadian goalie Ken Dryden would theorize years later, the Soviet Union needed to show that the kind of hockey they'd developed on their own — with soccer tactics and unprecedented physical conditioning as building blocks — was a viable way to play the game; Team Canada, meanwhile, simply and desperately needed to win the series for national pride. Both got what they needed, and in the years since, hockey has been the better for the integration of Russian philosophies within the more overtly physical North American game.

It was the first time the NHL's best (minus Bobby Hull and Bobby Orr) played the Soviet Union's best, and it marked Canada's return to international hockey after the Canadian Amateur Hockey Association stopped sending teams to the International Ice Hockey Federation (IIHF) World Championship in 1970 because it felt the ice surface was tilted. The Soviets, it was argued, were professional players in every sense of the word, continually overmatching the best amateurs Canada could send.

Because it was played when the Cold War was at its height, the series also became an athletic crusade for cultural validity: the familiar versus the other. Most Canadian hockey officials had predicted Canada would win easily, a notion that was bolstered by its early 2–0 lead in Game 1. But the early momentum soon gave way to total domination by the Soviets, and by the time the series was set to return to Moscow,

Canada had only a win and a tie, with a pair of losses, one of which prompted Phil Esposito's appeal for Canadians to appreciate how hard Team Canada was trying and how good the Soviets were.

When Canada lost Game 5 in Moscow, the situation became desperate for the Canadians, but Henderson's late scores gave Canada one-goal wins in the sixth and seventh games, setting up a winner-take-all eighth game.

It appeared that the series would end in a deadlock after Canada erased a two-goal deficit in the third period. Then, with the puck in the Soviet end in the final minute of play, Henderson did what he had never done in the NHL: summon a teammate off the ice because he wanted one more chance. The player he subbed in for, Pete Mahovlich, has said many times since that he was never so happy to be replaced.

The sequence that followed still resonates with all Canadian hockey fans of that era. Yvan Cournoyer gets the puck on the boards as Henderson charges to the net for the pass. Henderson reaches

for the pass but is upended by a defenseman and slides into the end boards. Phil Esposito retrieves the puck and whacks it towards Tretiak, who makes the save. The rebound comes to Henderson, who has recovered and is alone at the side of the net. Tretiak makes the initial save, and Henderson sweeps in the rebound.

"I jumped into Cournoyer's arms, the guys came pouring off the bench and the celebration was on," Henderson recalled. "My goodness, what a moment in time that was; I still get tingles thinking about it 40 years later."

Besides elation, the overwhelming feeling in the Canadian dressing room after the game was profound relief. Only the players knew how much pressure they'd been under and how they'd feared disappointing a nation.

"If we didn't win, we would've been known as losers for the rest of our lives," Henderson muses. "We felt it, but I think one of the reasons we did win was we never gave up hope, and when you have hope, there's a chance."

# Puck Luck Helps Set Unlikely Record

# DARRYL SITTLER

Darryl Sittler and Dave Reece on February 7, 1976.

No NHL player has ever been hotter. Not in a single game, anyway.

Darryl Sittler's 6 goals and 4 assists in Toronto's 11–4 victory over the Boston Bruins on February 7, 1976, gave him 2 more points than the previous standard set by Rocket Richard in 1944 and equaled a decade later by Richard's teammate Bert Olmstead. In the four decades since, ten more players have managed to record 8 points in a game, but none has registered 9, let alone 10.

"To see the number of players who've gone through the league, guys like Wayne Gretzky and Mario Lemieux — even today's players like Sidney Crosby — and I still hold the record," Sittler said in a CBC interview. "Who knows? At some point something might happen for some player where it may all come together. I'm proud to hold the record. I hope it lasts a lot longer."

As Sittler has pointed out, in today's lower-scoring NHL, it's rare for a team to score 10 goals in a game (between 1999–2000 and 2015–16, there were only 12 such games), so the chances of his record enduring for years to come are excellent.

More than any particular play, it's the sheer mass

of offense that made the night so memorable. But Sittler's final goal of the night captured the spirit of his record.

"I tried a pass-out from behind the net, and it struck the skates of two Boston players and went in," he said. "It was one of those 'when you're hot, you're hot' efforts.'"

The only goal he wasn't in on was George Ferguson's, from Inge Hammarstrom and Scott Garland.

Sittler's offensive explosion could not have been foreseen. The Leafs were only one game over .500, and Boston had come into Maple Leaf Gardens riding a seven-game winning streak and sporting a sizzling 15-1-1 record over the previous five weeks. Goaltender Dave Reece, a 27-year-old rookie, had played well, posting a 7-4-2 record in relief of Gilles Gilbert, but he had already been told he was heading back to the minors the next day because the Bruins had managed to re-sign Gerry Cheevers, who was returning after a three-and-a-half-year stint in the World Hockey Association.

As it turned out, Reece never played in the NHL

again, while Sittler went on to Hall of Fame honors.

The day before the eventful game, Harold Ballard, the crusty Leafs owner, singled Sittler out, telling the media that his team needed a better playmaker between wingers Lanny McDonald and Errol Thompson — even though Sittler, who had replaced Dave Keon as captain that season, was on his way to his first 100-point year.

"Undoubtedly, Mr. Ballard will figure his little blast inspired me to set the record, but it just isn't that way," Sittler insisted after the game.

Sittler says there was nothing different about the way he prepared for the game compared to the hundreds of others he played, except for his early-afternoon meal. Instead of the pasta he normally ate, he'd purchased barbecued chicken, which he wolfed down hurriedly in his car.

With his parents in Maple Leaf Gardens after he'd secured extra tickets from teammate Greg Hubick, Sittler assisted on goals by McDonald and defenseman Ian Turnbull in the first period. The onslaught began in earnest early in the second period when he scored from McDonald and Salming at 2:56 and then completed a hat trick and added 2 more assists over the next 11 minutes.

Between periods the game statistician told Sittler he was only 1 point away from the single-game points record, which he matched with his 4th goal of the game, just 44 seconds into the third period. Nine minutes later, he converted Thompson's pass for his 5th goal and his record-setting 9th point. He reached double digits with his double-ricochet goal with just over three minutes to play.

In an interview with *The Hockey News*, Sittler, who wore No. 27, pointed to the numerical karma riding shotgun with him.

"All the numbers were positive for me that night," he said. "We were playing on the seventh day of the second month, the Bruins were on a seven-game winning streak and we were in second place. The game started at 8:07 and officially ended at 10:27 p.m. I scored my first hat trick at the 10:27 mark of the second period and my 9th point at 9:27 of the third. Just coincidence, right? You'll never convince me."

It was the greatest single-game performance in league history. Not only did Sittler set the record for points in a game, but he also became the first NHL player to score 3 goals in back-to-back periods.

"It was a night when every time I had the puck, something seemed to happen," he told *The Hockey News*. "In other games, you work just as hard and come up empty."

# Pivotal Goal for Two Dynasties

# YVON LAMBERT

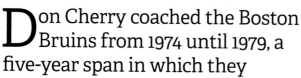

**D**on Cherry coached the Boston Bruins from 1974 until 1979, a five-year span in which they averaged 105 points a season. In 1976, Cherry was rewarded with the Jack Adams Award as the NHL's coach of the year. But while he and the Bruins came close during that run, they never managed to bring the Stanley Cup to Boston.

In 1977 and 1978, the Montreal Canadiens beat the Bruins in the Stanley Cup Final. In 1979 the two teams met again, this time in the semifinal. Many observers believed the winner of the series would ultimately take the Cup.

The heavily favored Canadiens won the first two games in Montreal, but the Bruins pushed back and won Games 3 and 4 in Boston. Each team again won on their home ice in Games 5 and 6, setting up Game 7 at the Montreal Forum on May 10, 1979.

The Bruins took a 3–1 lead into the third period on 2 goals by Wayne Cashman and 1 by Rick Middleton. They were 20 minutes from the Stanley Cup Final, but the Canadiens had confidence bred of success, along with nine future Hall of Famers in their lineup.

"We knew if we could get one goal, we'd get another," said the Canadiens' Doug Risebrough.

And they did. Mark Napier scored, and after Bruins defenseman Dick Redmond hooked Jacques Lemaire, Guy Lapointe tied the game with a shot from the point on the power play.

A Montreal victory seemed inevitable until Middleton scored his 2nd from a sharp angle, bouncing a backhand in off Ken Dryden's right arm with 3:59 left. That gave the Bruins a 4–3 lead.

"You want the buzzer to go. You want it to be over, but it goes on and on and on," said Bruins goalie Gilles Gilbert, who had taken over from Gerry Cheevers in Game 3 and won three of the next four games, earning the game's first star twice.

With the game winding down, Montreal coach Scotty Bowman double-shifted Guy Lafleur. Whatever the reason — an attempt to match lines, the noise of the crowd or the intervention of the ghosts of the Forum — the Bruins were called for having too many men on the ice with 2:34 remaining.

"That was my fault," said Cherry. "They must have thought they heard me say something. I had to grab two other guys, or we'd have had eight out there!"

Writing in *Sports Illustrated*, Michael Farber called the infraction "the most significant penalty in the history of major sports in North America."

Moments later Lemaire dropped the puck to Lafleur who let go a low, powerful slap shot that blew past Gilbert.

"The shot was so hard it hydroplaned, hitting the ice and skipping over the pad," said Napier. "I don't know any goalie then or now who would have stopped it."

Eight minutes into overtime, Gilbert made a spectacular save on Shutt — the Canadiens' 50th shot of the game.

A minute later, Mario Tremblay skated down the right wing with defenseman Al Sims alongside. On the left side, Yvon Lambert headed for the net, arriving just in time to meet Tremblay's pass. He deflected the puck into the net and ended the series at 9:33 of overtime.

"The first time I had the chance to score, I went in too deep," said Lambert. "The puck got mixed up in my skates. This time when I saw Mario with the puck, I put my head down and said, 'I don't care … I'm getting there.' I wasn't thinking about anything else. The pass was a perfect one. The goalie had no chance. It was over."

Gilbert was named the first star of the game, but it was cold comfort.

"Usually, hockey players man up, but enough tears flowed in our dressing room to fill an ocean," said the Bruins' Mike Milbury. "In the room. On the flight home. There was a complete breakdown of emotions. We were confronted with the realization of how close we had come to a lifelong dream. And we had to recognize it was our own fault. We were one penalty away from wearing rings."

The Canadiens went on to capture their fourth straight Stanley Cup. After the final, Lemaire, Dryden and Yvan Cournoyer retired, and Bowman, who had won five Cups in seven seasons in Montreal, left to coach the Buffalo Sabres. Their dynasty was over.

Two weeks after Game 7 in Montreal, Cherry was fired. In 1980 he made his first appearance on *Hockey Night in Canada*, and his Coach's Corner segment is now a national institution.

During the segment's introduction, Cherry can be seen at the Forum, gesturing to rival fans. It's his signature moment behind the bench, during the game in which Lafleur, Lambert and *Les Glorieux* ended his tenure as Boston's coach.

# Do You Believe in Miracles?

## MIKE ERUZIONE

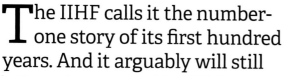

Τhe IIHF calls it the number-one story of its first hundred years. And it arguably will still be the number-one story of the IIHF's first *two* hundred years. What could ever top it?

It has an iconic nickname — Miracle on Ice — that sprung from one of the most memorable TV calls in sport: Al Michaels' "Do you believe in miracles? Yes!" It was commandeered into a cultural symbol of freedom triumphing over oppression and eventually stimulated the growth of the United States into one of the world's great hockey powers.

"People will come up to me and say, 'Hey, I remember where I was when we won that game.' And I say, 'We?'" Eruzione laughed in recollection.

"But that's what it felt like for people. Around the country, and for others around the world, it was a good-versus-evil thing. But for us, it was just a hockey game."

In February 1980, the Soviet Union had already invaded Afghanistan, American hostages were still being held captive in Iran and the U.S. economy was struggling, but nobody expected that a Friday afternoon game at the Olympic Fieldhouse in downtown Lake Placid, New York, would become the patriotic rallying cry a nation needed. On the contrary, the game wasn't even shown on live television.

"I think in 1980, Americans were looking for something to feel good about, and that happened to be us," Eruzione says. "We showed that, despite the obstacles and the odds, we can do anything."

The Soviet Union's hockey team was sequestered for 11 months a year and had won every Olympic gold medal since it entered the tournament in 1956, save for another American upset at Squaw Valley, California, in 1960. The hyperskilled Big Red Machine played in five-man units and was regarded in North America as a pro team, but a faceless, monolithic one. The U.S. team was a collection of talented but inexperienced college players and minor pro prospects, such as the 25-year-old Eruzione, who had played at Boston University and then for Toledo in the International Hockey League.

And 13 days prior to the game in question (what was essentially the Olympic semifinal), the Soviets hammered the Americans, 10–3, in a pre-tournament tune-up at Madison Square Garden.

Left: Mike Eruzione falls while shooting against Finland.
Right: Team USA celebrates Eruzione's winning goal against the Soviets in 1980.

But the Americans opened the Olympic tournament with an emotional statement, rallying with 27 seconds left for a tie with Sweden. The U.S. side hadn't beaten the Swedes in 20 years, and the tie provided the Americans some confidence. After that the host team went undefeated over seven more games, including the final two: 4–3 over the Soviets and 4–2 over Finland two days later to give them the most shocking gold medal in Olympic hockey history.

The Americans trailed in six of their seven games, including three times in the Soviet game. But twice Mark Johnson, the Americans' top skater in the Olympics, tied the game, including at 2–2 with one second left in the first period. That compelled Soviet coach Viktor Tikhonov to pull legendary goalie Vladislav Tretiak in favor of Vladimir Myshkin, sending a jolt of confidence across the American bench. Years later, Tikhonov would say it was the biggest mistake of his coaching career.

Johnson's goal at 8:39 of the third again erased a Soviet lead, and a minute later Eruzione jumped on the ice as Buzz Schneider dumped the puck from the blue line to Myshkin, who played it to his right. But two Soviet defenders couldn't control it, and Matt Pavelich tipped the puck towards the middle of the ice, where Eruzione pounced on it and unleashed the shot heard around the hockey world.

"I think their defenseman was screening the goalie," a still-dazed Eruzione said after the game. "I don't think [Myshkin] saw it. I still can't believe this has happened."

While Johnson led the team in scoring and goalie Jim Craig stopped 36 of 39 Soviet shots (the Americans had only 19), it's Eruzione's goal that most people associate with the Miracle on Ice, particularly his joyful sprint on the tips of his skates towards a crush of welcoming teammates.

Many of the players on the American team that won the 1996 World Cup, the next significant international triumph for the United States, said they had been inspired to take up or stay in the game by the 1980 team.

"There aren't many sporting events that touched the lives of a country like ours did, especially in the sport of ice hockey," said Eruzione on the 35th anniversary of his goal. "To think that a moment can capture the spirit of a nation is something my teammates and I take great pride knowing we were a part of.

"I've said many times, in '80 we may have opened the door. Today's players have knocked the door down. It's great to see the success of our programs."

In the arena parking lot after the game, Eruzione was asked by a reporter about the feeling he "could not describe." Had it been ecstasy?

"That's not strong enough," he answered. "We beat the Russians. *We beat the Russians.*"

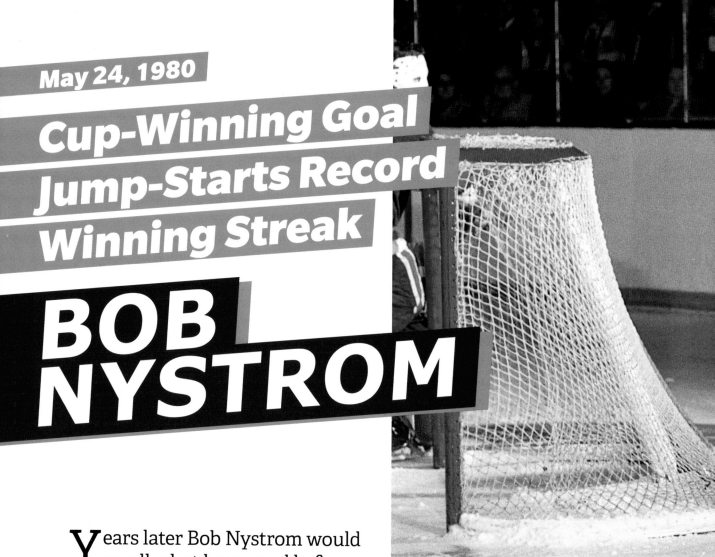

## May 24, 1980

# Cup-Winning Goal Jump-Starts Record Winning Streak

# BOB NYSTROM

Years later Bob Nystrom would recall what happened before the game with as much relish as he recalled what ended it.

"In the warmup, the crowd was as loud as any crowd I've ever played in front of," he said of the afternoon of May 24, 1980, when the New York Islanders prepared to play the Philadelphia Flyers in Game 6 of the Stanley Cup Final at Nassau Veterans Memorial Coliseum.

"I had chills running up and down my spine and almost broke out in tears while I was skating around, trying to get ready for the game," says Nystrom, who, hours later, scored at 7:11 of overtime to give the Islanders the first of their four straight Stanley Cups. "The fans stood on their feet and cheered continuously for the entire warmup.

"And the ending of the game wasn't that bad, either."

Before Nystrom's goal gave the Isles their 3–2 victory, the game seemed destined to be remembered more for linesman Leon Stickle's blown offside call in regulation time, which allowed Duane Sutter's

goal — and a 2–1 Islander lead — to stand. Stickle admitted he had missed the call. Thankfully, the Flyers scored, and the outcome was left in the hands of the players.

The winning sequence began when Nystrom engaged three Flyers behind the Islanders' goal line and forced a weak clearing pass, which Lorne Henning eventually corralled before sending a perfect lead pass to John Tonelli, who was breaking out of the Islanders' zone. As Tonelli crossed the line and encountered Philadelphia's André Dupont, he pulled the puck to his forehand and fed it to his left, to the streaking Nystrom. With all the speed he'd built up joining the play from behind his own goal line, all Nystrom had to do with Tonelli's crisp pass was redirect it, which he did from his backhand and past Pete Peeters for the biggest goal in Islanders history.

"It was absolutely amazing to watch it go in," Nystrom recalls.

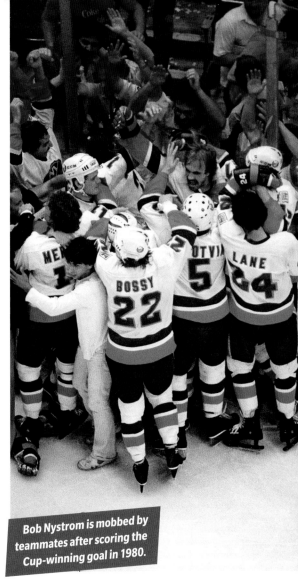

Bob Nystrom is mobbed by teammates after scoring the Cup-winning goal in 1980.

Tonelli and Henning were the first to reach Nystrom as he leapt up and down in the left-hand corner, and that was one hugely symbolic hug fest. The three composed New York's third line, and none of them would be among the six players and one coach that the Islanders dynasty would eventually send to the Hockey Hall of Fame. Nystrom's game was that of a grinder, but he did come up with a number of big goals. Mike Bossy always said it was fitting that one of the team's important foot soldiers should score the goal to finally put the Isles over the top.

It had been a long, long climb that had stalled far too often. Starting in their third season, the talented Islanders lost three straight semifinals to the eventual Cup champions (the Philadelphia Flyers and, twice, the Montreal Canadiens) and then were upset by the Toronto Maple Leafs and New York Rangers in 1978 and '79, before Nystrom's goal finally removed that stain of underachievement. *Sports Illustrated* said Nystrom's goal "gave the New York Islanders a whole new image. They are the Stanley Cup champi-

ons now, not a bunch of chokers."

It was as if a stubborn cork had just been popped. Starting with the four rounds they won in the spring of 1980, the Islanders would win 19 consecutive post-season series before the Edmonton Oilers beat them in the 1984 Cup Final to begin their own memorable run. Many hockey analysts say the string of series wins is one of the NHL records that will likely never be broken, and Hall of Famer Bryan Trottier has said the undefeated streak was his team's most significant achievement.

With the victory, the Islanders became the second expansion-era team to win the Cup — Philadelphia being the first. Nystrom's decisive goal was the last NHL play seen on U.S. network television for a full decade, and it put an end to early-afternoon games in the Stanley Cup Final.

It also put an end to the Islanders' near decade of frustration and finally put the first suburban Stanley Cup winners on an equal footing with the neighboring New York Rangers.

# April 30, 1986

# Own Goal Threatened to Derail Dynasty

## STEVE SMITH

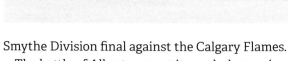

How did Steve Smith respond when Mark Messier asked him to go out for a drink?

"I don't know. I'll have to bounce it off Grant Fuhr first."

Thirty years later, Steve Smith can laugh at jokes like that. As a matter of fact, he's always been able to see the humor in one of the greatest gaffes in Stanley Cup playoff history. Even minutes after the game, though he'd been crying in the handshake line and at his locker in the bowels of Northlands Coliseum while the media grilled him, the first-year NHLer found it in himself to crack a joke: "I got good wood on it. I thought it went in fast."

Smith, a tall, rugged, mobile defenseman who actually started as a right-winger, worked his way up through the Oilers system and joined the club in 1985–86. He was an excellent plus-30 in the regular season, but a healthy scratch for four playoff games. On a very deep team, it took a Lee Fogolin injury for Smith to suit up for the biggest game of the season.

April 30, 1986, was Smith's 23rd birthday. And that night he and his Oilers teammates — including superstars Wayne Gretzky, Mark Messier, Paul Coffey and Grant Fuhr — were to play Game 7 of the

Smythe Division final against the Calgary Flames.

The battle of Alberta was at its peak that spring. Two years earlier the Flames had taken the Oilers to seven games in the Smythe Division final. Edmonton ultimately won that series, and, later, their first Stanley Cup, which they successfully defended in 1985. With as potent an offense as the game had ever seen and all their key players in the prime of their careers, Edmonton seemed an unstoppable force and the NHL's next dynasty.

About 300 kilometers down Highway 2, the Flames had also built a solid roster with their own future Hall of Famers and legendary coach "Badger Bob" Johnson at the helm. By the 1986 playoffs, the Flames had become an immovable object, with a physical team and a system that stymied scorers.

Edmonton's bid for a three-peat was in serious doubt as the series went the distance. Calgary took a 2–0 lead in Game 7 — played in Edmonton — but the Oilers came back to tie it.

Throughout the series, the Oilers had tried long cross-ice passes to catch the Flames off guard on a

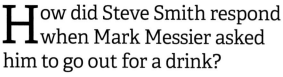

line change and break down their defensive system. Several times in Game 7, Coffey had thrown the puck across the crease, something the broadcasters took note of in the second period.

With five minutes gone in the third, Fuhr settled the puck for Smith behind his net. As Fuhr returned to his crease a little too casually, Smith saw the Flames changing and went for the long pass. It hit the back of Fuhr's leg and went into the net. Fans in the arena and watching on TV had no idea why the goal light was on. Then the realization and shock set in.

"Oh, they scored!" exclaimed sportscaster Don Wittman. "Oh, Steve Smith, in attempting to get it out of his own zone, put it into his own net!"

Smith started to skate back to the bench but simply collapsed on the ice, the full weight of what had happened bearing down on him.

While the blame fell on Smith, the Oilers — the second-highest scoring team in NHL history, averaging more than five goals a game in the regular season — couldn't tie the score in the 14 minutes and 43 seconds that remained. So Smith wore the horns and has lived with them ever since.

It wasn't all bad, however.

"It taught me humility," says Smith. "I came into Edmonton as a brash, young guy. It taught me to cheer for people. To expect — and want — good out of people as I moved forward in life.

"I never wanted anyone to have the day that I had that day. And that's something I've stuck to pretty closely for a long, long time. I am a much more positive person now than ever."

The Flames went on to the Stanley Cup Final, where they lost to rookie sensation Patrick Roy and the Montreal Canadiens. The Oilers won three of the next four titles, with Calgary winning the other in 1989.

After Gretzky, as the Oilers' captain, lifted the Cup in 1987, the first person he handed it to was Smith. The 111th overall pick wasn't even the first Steve Smith to be drafted in 1981, but he won more Stanley Cups — three — than anyone selected in his draft year.

Smith's long and distinguished career came to an end in 2000, when he retired as a member of the Calgary Flames.

## Easter Epic

# PAT LaFONTAINE

Hardly a day goes by that Pat LaFontaine doesn't hear from a hockey fan or two about how they spent the first two hours of their Easter Sunday in 1987.

And he still describes the entire Saturday evening — and parts of the morning that followed — as "surreal."

The New York Islanders center, positioned alone and uncovered at the Washington Capitals' blue line, wheeled and blindly fired the puck in a way he says he never did again in his career. The seeing-eye shot found its way past potential shot-blockers and a screen by the Isles' Dale Henry, caromed off the post and beat goalie Bob Mason for a memorable 3–2 New York victory.

That stopped the clock, with 8:47 remaining in the fourth overtime, at 1:58 a.m., six hours and 18 minutes after the opening faceoff. The game was immediately dubbed the Easter Epic.

The goal was memorable not only because it was scored in Game 7 of the opening round of the playoffs but also because the Islanders became just the third team in Stanley Cup history to rebound from a 3-1 deficit to claim a series. At the time, the only other such rallies had been executed by the 1942 Toronto Maple Leafs and by the Islanders themselves in 1975 (both teams had improbably clawed their way out of a 3-0 hole).

It was also the first game since 1971 to last into a third overtime, and the first since 1951 — a span of 36 years — to require a fourth. Except for veteran Islander goalie Billy Smith, no player on either roster had been born when Maurice Richard ended the 1951 Montreal-Detroit tilt that required four extra frames.

As for LaFontaine, the only thing on his mind was shooting the puck.

"I just wanted to shoot it and hope for the best, because everything Kelly Hrudey and Bob Mason saw, they stopped," LaFontaine told *The Hockey News*.

"I remember the puck being off on its side, so I didn't catch it flat, and it kind of knuckled."

LaFontaine heard the puck hit the post and didn't realize he'd scored until his weary teammates started to rush toward him.

"And then it was just unbelievable emotion for

about a minute. Then we just all collapsed."

As much out of exhaustion as joy.

New York was playing without big-time contributors Mike Bossy, Denis Potvin and Brent Sutter because of injuries, and the Capitals looked to take advantage. But Hrudey's stellar play in net kept the Islanders in it for long stretches when they were being outplayed. LaFontaine's shot was the Islanders' 57th of the game, while the Capitals, who never trailed in the game until the second it ended, directed a stunning 75 shots at Hrudey, who was in the net that series and in 12 of New York's playoff games instead of Smith that spring.

With fatigue setting in for the players and the fans, LaFontaine says, that when he looked into the stands just before he came onto the ice for his fateful shot, "I saw people sleeping.

"Our equipment man [Jim Pickard] told me he thought I was going to pop one. And then the organ player in the arena started playing the theme from *The Twilight Zone*. The whole thing was just surreal."

The play leading up to the goal unfolded matter-of-factly. New York defenseman Ken Leiter — in whose vacated spot LaFontaine eventually found himself — rushed the puck in the Capitals' end for a chance on net. He didn't score, and Islanders teammate Gord Dineen then circled the net with the puck. But his shot was blocked by Kevin Hatcher and caromed on an angle back to LaFontaine on the right side of the blue line. LaFontaine's unrehearsed quick spin and fire sent what was left of the crowd at the Capital Centre home into a collective sleep-deprived depression.

The Islanders' marathon win gave the franchise both the longest and shortest overtime wins in an elimination game in Stanley Cup history. New York had sidelined the crosstown Rangers after just 11 seconds of overtime in the third game of their preliminary-round series in 1975.

The 1987 Islanders went on to play the Flyers in the Patrick Division final, again fell behind three games to one and again forced a seventh game, but this time they were soundly defeated, 5–1.

# 1987 Canada Cup Championship

# GRETZKY TO LEMIEUX

For a generation too young to remember the 1972 Summit Series, Canada Cup '87 was the best hockey ever played, with the best team that Canada ever iced. It was also the end of an era.

The rivalry between Canada and the Soviet Union that had been born in '72 was alive and well in 1987. Earlier that year a game between the two nations at the World Junior Hockey Championship in Czechoslovakia devolved into a bench-clearing brawl that came to be known as the Punch-up in Piestany. The on-ice officials, unable to control the players, left the ice, and the arena lights were turned off. Both teams were banished from the tournament.

Traditionally, meetings between these rivals pitted the Soviets' skill and systems against the heart and grit of Team Canada. But this time Canada could boast five future Hall of Famers on the power play and a roster so deep that a number of future Hall of Famers — Steve Yzerman, Patrick Roy, Cam Neely, Scott Stevens and Al MacInnis — didn't make the cut.

Wayne Gretzky was 26 and in his prime but reluctant to sign on after a grueling season that culminated in Edmonton's third Stanley Cup. Mario Lemieux, at 21, was just entering his prime.

But the Soviets could respond in kind with the famed KLM line — Vladimir Krutov, Igor Larionov and Sergei Makarov — and Viacheslav Fetisov on defense. And they still played a style of hockey foreign to Canadians, with fluidity and grace that comes only through playing together since childhood. The Soviet system developed the country's best young players and kept them together with CSKA Moscow, popularly known as the Red Army team. In an exhibition game prior to the Canada Cup, the Soviets dismissed Canada with ease by a lopsided 9–4 margin.

"There's no question, at the time, they were the best team in the world," says Gretzky.

Canada took some time to come together when the tournament started. In the round robin, they tied Czechoslovakia, 4–4, and the Soviet Union, 3–3. Facing the Czechs again in the semifinal, Canada fell behind 2–0 but rallied for a 5–3 win to set up a best-of-three final against the Soviets.

It looked as though the Big Red Machine was going to steamroll Canada in Game 1 on September 11 at the Montreal Forum. The Soviets had a 4–1 lead in

*Mario Lemieux celebrates the dramatic winning goal in the 1987 Canada Cup.*

utes left, the Soviets had a faceoff in Canada's zone.

Dale Hawerchuk lost the faceoff but won the battle, and Lemieux poked the puck past the defenseman to set up a 2-on-1, with Gretzky and Larry Murphy bearing down on Igor Kravchuk. Murphy headed for the front of the net, while Gretzky crossed the blue line along the left boards, waiting for the trailing Lemieux.

"Murphy without question made the goal possible," says Gretzky. "He went to the net, and in going to the net, he took the defenseman all the way to the goaltender. Mario was left wide open."

And Lemieux made no mistake, firing a wrist shot over the glove of goalie Sergei Mylnikov.

According to Murphy: "I was wide open right at the corner of the net, and I thought it was coming for sure. I think the goalie thought it was too, so he was leaning my way, and Mario fired it in the other direction. He had the corner and he doesn't miss those. I was just happy it was in the net, to be perfectly honest."

The arena and country erupted, and Canada held the fort for the final 1:26 to win the game — 6–5, of course — and the series, 2-1.

Two hockey superpowers, separated by one goal after three games. A winning goal put together by two of the most gifted offensive players in the history of the game. It was Lemieux's 11th goal in nine tournament games, including four game-winners, and Gretzky's 18th assist and tournament-record 21st point. It was the last time the duo ever played together for Canada.

The Berlin Wall fell in 1989, and after the Iron Curtain was drawn back, there was a steady influx of players from the former Soviet Union to the NHL. While the Canada-Russia rivalry remains passionate, the mystery and geopolitical undercurrent that permeated 1972 and 1987 have faded into history.

Canada Cup '87 featured hockey at its finest, punctuated by three words — "Gretzky to Lemieux" — that became shorthand for victory. Words that joined Foster Hewitt's "Henderson has scored for Canada" in the hockey lexicon and still send shivers down the spine of any Canadian lucky enough to have witnessed the goal.

"It was a tremendous sense of accomplishment," reminisced Murphy almost 30 years later. "It was the end of good versus evil, the last of the Soviet Union. It was a historic event. You could feel it at the time."

the second period, but Canada fought back to tie it at 5 before Alexander Semak scored in overtime to give the Soviets a 6–5 win and the series lead.

Games 2 and 3 were played at Hamilton's Copps Coliseum. Canada had a 3–1 advantage heading into the first intermission of Game 2, but the Soviets evened it up at 3 after 40 minutes. In the third period, Canada took the lead twice, but the Soviets answered back each time, including a brilliant individual effort by Valeri Kamensky to tie the game with 1:04 left.

It took until 10:04 of the second overtime period to decide the game. After Grant Fuhr kept Canada in it with a series of spectacular saves, Gretzky set up Lemieux for his 3rd goal of the game and Gretzky's 5th point. Another 6–5 game tied the series.

With one game to decide the winner of the tournament and crown the world's greatest hockey nation, the Soviets came out flying on September 15. They built a 3–0 lead eight minutes into the game, but Canada responded and led 5–4 after two periods. Semak tied it at 12:21 of the third, and with less than two min-

# 1,851 Points & 802 Goals

# WAYNE GRETZKY

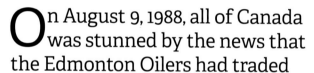

On August 9, 1988, all of Canada was stunned by the news that the Edmonton Oilers had traded Wayne Gretzky, Marty McSorley and Mike Krushelnyski to the Los Angeles Kings for Jimmy Carson, Martin Gélinas, first-round draft picks in 1989, 1991 and 1993, and $15 million in cash. This was before the advent of chattering panels of "insiders" on sports TV networks and online platforms such as Twitter, and there had been no rumors or leaks in advance of the announcement, only bold headlines that the country's favorite son was leaving for America's entertainment and celebrity capital.

The Edmonton Oilers had just won their fourth Stanley Cup in five years, and Gretzky had earned his second Conn Smythe Trophy as playoff MVP. The team's many stars were in the prime of their careers and seemed poised to win many more, led by the Great One.

Gretzky had married actress Janet Jones just weeks prior, so she took the initial brunt of the country's anger, seen as the Yoko Ono to the Edmonton Beatles. The blame was misplaced. At the time, Oilers owner Peter Pocklington was out of money, and Kings owner Bruce McNall had plenty of it. Mc-

Nall's fortune turned out to be smoke and mirrors, however, and he was sent to prison for fraud and conspiracy in 1997.

Asked in 2013 whether a similar trade could happen again, McNall responded: "No chance. No chance that it can happen again. In part, the league would never allow a team to buy a player the way I did and guise it as a trade. Also, there is not a player [who] could have the same effect Gretzky had at that time in this day and age. There is a difference between the best player currently and the best player ever."

With the Oilers, Gretzky had set many of his unassailable records, including goals (92), assists (163) and points (215) in a season, not to mention his scoring 50 goals in the first 39 games in 1981–82. But he wasn't in Edmonton long enough to break Gordie Howe's all-time records. Those marks would be surpassed with the Great One wearing Los Angeles' new black and silver uniform.

In a script that could've been written in Hollywood — which lies just a few miles north of the Kings' home arena at the time, the Great Western Forum —

16, 1960. "He's good, and I know, because I played with him. If you want to tell me he's the greatest player of all time, I have no argument at all."

Gretzky demurred. "See, one of the great things about [Howe] is that he doesn't get into comparing eras. You'll never get him to say that the competition now is watered down."

A year after leading the Kings to the franchise's first Stanley Cup Final appearance, in 1993 — they lost to the Montreal Canadiens — Gretzky was approaching Howe's record of 801 goals. The march to the top was inexorable, but it was also becoming painful.

In March 1994 the struggling Kings were out of playoff contention. Gretzky's home had been damaged in an earthquake earlier in the season, his friend and business partner John Candy had just died, and he had the flu. He had scored only 1 goal in seven games, but maybe he wanted to sit on 799 for a while and let his idol hold the top spot for a bit longer.

There's a famous photo of Howe, at the height of his considerable powers, drawing in an adolescent and starstruck Gretzky with the crook of his stick.

"The first time I met him, I was 10 years old, and my dad said to me, 'How was it meeting Mr. Howe?' and I said, 'It was the greatest day of my life.'"

Gretzky was back in Edmonton on October 15, 1989, with the chance to break Howe's career record of 1,850 points. It had taken Howe 26 seasons to amass that total. Gretzky was in his 11th.

You don't set records without a little luck, but Gretzky tended to make his own. With the clock winding down and Kings goalie Mario Gosselin pulled for an extra skater, the puck bounced off teammate Dave Taylor's leg and right to Gretzky, who always seemed to be in the right spot at the most important time. He put it behind Oilers goalie Bill Ranford to tie the game and earn his 1,851st point. The Edmonton fans, who had never really blamed Gretzky for the trade, erupted.

"I don't know what made me go there," Gretzky said after the game. "I'm usually the outlet guy."

With a flair for the dramatic, Gretzky also scored the overtime winner in the 5–4 victory.

"I kissed that record goodbye a long time ago, when Wayne started getting 200 points a year," said Howe, almost 30 years after he passed Maurice Richard's high-water mark of 946 points on January

Although they played very different games — one relied on force, the other finesse — Gretzky did emulate Howe's humility and respect for the game and its fans. By the time he was reeling in Howe's records, the two had become close friends.

On March 20 in San Jose, Gretzky scored goals 800 and 801, the second a rebound of his own shot with 49 seconds left that tied the score at 6. It had taken Gretzky 1,116 games to get to 801, compared to 1,767 for Howe.

At home against the Vancouver Canucks on March 23, Gretzky became the greatest goal-scorer in NHL history. Number 802 was scored on the power play at 14:47 of the second period, into a virtually empty net, after Canucks goalie Kirk McLean overplayed McSorley, who set up Gretzky.

Asked about his role in the record-breaker, McSorley said, "I just count my blessing that I've been able to play with him for eight-plus years."

Gretzky, who scored his first NHL goal against Vancouver, celebrated with an impromptu dance, and the game was halted for an on-ice ceremony with his parents, his wife, McNall and NHL commissioner Gary Bettman.

"I always tell people I base records on which ones are the hardest to break," Gretzky said, when asked to rank his. "Fifty goals in 39 games, 163 assists, 51

straight games with a point, 802 goals. Those will be the hardest to break; 802 will be tough. That's 50 goals for 16 years. That's a lot of games."

Gretzky retired with 2,857 points and 61 official NHL records. Take away his 894 career goals, and his 1,963 assists would still be enough to rank him as the NHL's all-time points leader. "Ten years from now, they won't talk about my goal scoring," he said. "It'll just be my passing."

It's been more than a decade since his last game and his Hall of Fame induction — both in 1999, naturally — and his goal-scoring exploits and uncanny setups remain legendary. And in the modern NHL, his all-time records seem even more untouchable.

"Yet it's the man, not the record-breaker, that the NHL will most miss," wrote E.M. Swift after Gretzky's last game. "He is the sport's only transcendent star, but his deep love of the game is still farm boy simple."

The parallels are inescapable. Howe called himself "just a lucky old farm boy," and, despite the numbers, Gretzky still believes Gordie was the best to ever lace up.

"He was a special person, he was a great ambassador for the game of hockey, he was a great father and great grandfather," eulogized Gretzky when Howe died in 2016.

"To me, he was the greatest hockey player who

# Rookie Goal Record First Highlight in Storied Career

# TEEMU SELANNE

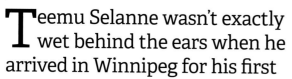

Teemu Selanne wasn't exactly wet behind the ears when he arrived in Winnipeg for his first NHL season. The Jets had drafted him 10th overall in 1988 but chose to let him develop his game against players in Finland's top professional league, with Helsinki's Jokerit.

After playing for Finland at the Olympics in Albertville, France, and winning the Finnish league title and the Aarne Honkavaara Trophy as the league's top goal-scorer in 1992, Selanne was ready to make the move to North America.

By that time, Selanne was a group four (restricted) free agent, and the Calgary Flames offered him $1.5 million more than Winnipeg had. But the Jets weren't willing to let him walk; they matched the offer.

"I think he was really determined, coming over under that sort of pressure," said Selanne's agent, Don Baizley, who was a father figure to the right-winger. "He was going to prove to people that he was a good player. It wasn't the offer sheet so much as the reaction to the offer sheet."

Also on hand in Winnipeg to help ease Selanne's transition to a new country, team and league were veteran defenseman Teppo Numminen and assistant coach Alpo Suhonen.

"When I first got there, I didn't know much about Winnipeg," says Selanne. "I know there are two things: hockey and great people."

The 22-year-old scored 3 goals in his fifth NHL game and 11 goals in his first 12 outings. The Jets, however, were 5-12-1 in the first month of the season. The team was laden with rookies, and losing got to Selanne. He was thrown out of a game against the Montreal Canadiens after swinging a high stick, but the season turned for him on December 28 when Eddie Olczyk was traded to the New York Rangers for Tie Domi and Kris King.

The two tough guys opened up space and looked after Selanne, and it would be nine years before he earned his next game misconduct.

After the trade, the Jets went 11-1-2, with an eight-game goal streak by Selanne spurring an eight-game winning streak. At the end of January 1993, the Jets were above .500, and Selanne — the "Finnish Flash" — had 40 goals. The eyes of the hockey world were

now on Winnipeg and the league's new superstar.

At that point the New York Islanders' Mike Bossy, arguably the purest goal-scorer in NHL history, owned — for 15 years — the rookie record of 53 goals. Many thought it would be his for far longer, especially after Selanne slowed down a little in February. By February 28, Selanne had 47 goals but had gone three straight games without scoring, his longest drought since the opening month of the season. The assumption was that the long NHL season and the travel had worn Selanne down.

Playing at home against the Minnesota North Stars that night, Selanne exploded for 4 goals, breaking the magical 50-goal barrier and making the record inevitable. Only two nights later, on March 2, he scored 3 goals against the Quebec Nordiques, and the record was his. He punctuated number 54 — a one-handed goal on a partial breakaway — by throwing his glove in the air and shooting it down with his stick. The old record was dead; long live King Teemu.

It took Selanne just 64 games to score 54 times, and the record-breaker was one of 11 goals he scored over a five-game stretch. He added 20 more in March, including a nine-game scoring streak, and at the end of the season, he had 76 goals, 56 assists and 132 points. He was the unanimous choice for the Calder Trophy as rookie of the year, and he was sixth in Hart Trophy voting for league MVP.

In February 1996, the Jets traded Selanne to the Anaheim Ducks, and in 2007 the team won the Stanley Cup. He played three years with the San Jose Sharks and one with the Colorado Avalanche between two stints with the Ducks.

Selanne retired in 2014 at the age of 43, with 684 goals, 773 assists and 1,457 points in 1,451 career games. In 2015 the Ducks retired Selanne's No. 8 — the first in team history to be so honored. He's the Anaheim franchise leader in goals, assists, points and games played, and he holds one of the NHL's seemingly unbreakable records.

Barring radical rule changes like increasing the size of the nets, hockey may never see another 76-goal scorer, let alone one in his first year in the NHL. The most goals any rookie has scored since Selanne broke the record was 52, by Alexander Ovechkin in 2005–06, and only two players of any description have reached 60 in the last 20 years: Ovechkin, with 65 in 2007–08, and Steven Stamkos, with 60 in 2011–12.

The Finnish national team also retired Selanne's number after he dedicated 26 years of hockey to his country, a span that included four Olympic medals — one silver and three bronze — over six Olympics.

# February 27, 1994

## Shoot-Out Goal Scores Lillehammer Gold

# PETER FORSBERG

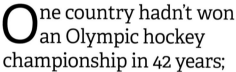

Peter Forsberg celebrates his amazing shoot-out goal (right) in 1994.

O ne country hadn't won an Olympic hockey championship in 42 years; the other had never won it. So whichever way the 1994 gold-medal game in Lillehammer, Norway, turned out, it was going to be memorable.

But nobody — certainly not the Swedish postal service — could have predicted how memorable or why.

On February 27, 1994, Canada and Sweden battled their way through 60 minutes of entertaining, physical hockey and 10 tense minutes of overtime before beginning a five-player shoot-out round to determine which hockey power would finally snap its long Olympic gold-medal drought.

Each team scored twice in its first five shots. Petr Nedved and 19-year-old Paul Kariya had given Canada a 2–0 edge before Magnus Svensson and 20-year-old Peter Forsberg evened it up for Sweden. That necessitated a sudden-death round, and both Nedved and Svensson missed on their respective teams' first attempts.

As the shoot-out went to seventh shots, Swedish coach Curt Lundmark wanted one of Hakan Loob or Mats Naslund, each of whom had missed in the

earlier shoot-out round, to take the next attempt. But neither of the former Stanley Cup champions wanted to be thrust into that boiling cauldron of pressure. So Forsberg, who had set the World Junior Championship scoring record the year before, got the nod.

"The coach tapped those guys on the shoulder, and they said no," recalls Canada's head coach, Tom Renney. "He then tapped Peter, and he went over the boards and scored the goal. That's rising to the occasion."

Canadian goalie Corey Hirsch had also been rising to the occasion throughout the tournament, and like Forsberg, he hadn't been his coach's first choice in the sudden-death shoot-out. Prior to the game, the Canadian coaching staff had decided that if a shoot-out should be required, they'd switch to Manny Legace because he was viewed as slightly better at stopping penalty shots. But Legace bruised a knee during warmup.

The left shooting Forsberg's first shoot-out goal had come off a deke to the left and a move to the

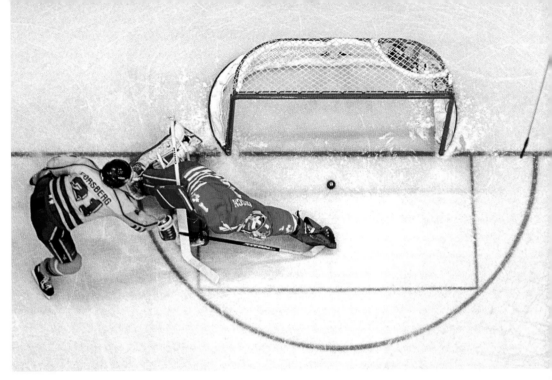

right, and as he bore down on Hirsch the second time, he started at the right post and drifted to the left again. The Canadian goalie tracked him perfectly, and as Forsberg moved in so tight, Hirsch has said he thought he had him.

But at the last second, Forsberg, who by then was on top of the crease at an arms' length from the post, swiveled and opened his body up to the net. With only his right hand on the stick, he reached and pushed the puck back across the front of the net to the right side while his body continued to drift left. Hirsh, who was helplessly sliding away from the puck and into the path of Forsberg's body, reached desperately with his glove to cover the vacated side of the net. But the puck slid mere inches under his outstretched glove and into the goal.

Thus, on the second-last shot of the Olympics, was the legend of the Forsberg goal born.

Canada still had one more chance, but Tommy Salo made a brilliant save on Kariya to send Sweden into national euphoria.

"No one had really seen that in Olympic competition," Hirsch said. "Or in any competition. No one had ever seen a move like that."

Well actually, Forsberg had. He said he'd patterned the move on Kent Nilsson's shoot-out goal against the United States' John Vanbiesbrouck at the 1989 world championship. And, seconds after Forsberg scored, the Swedish TV commentators mentioned Nilsson.

"But I didn't really make it right," Forsberg said. "By the time I drew my stick back, I was too far to the left side of the net."

Still, as Hirsch would later say, "Great players find a way to make great plays."

When PostNord Sverige, the Swedish postal service, wanted to issue a stamp to commemorate the occasion, Hirsch said the goal embarrassed him, and he refused permission for his likeness to be used. So on the resulting stamp, issued in 1995, Hirsch's name was removed from the back of his sweater, the sweater was colored blue instead of Canadian red, and his number was changed from 1 to 11.

Hirsch, only 21 at the time, later explained that he was young and had been given some bad advice. In time he would come to view the goal differently. It helped that whenever the goal was remembered, the focus was overwhelmingly on Forsberg's brilliant play and not on a Hirsch mistake (he'd almost made the save). Plus he had an Olympic silver medal.

The Lillehammer games were the last Olympics before NHL players were allowed to take part, and Canada's young team was vastly less experienced — especially in shoot-outs, which weren't a major part of North America's hockey fabric. Still, the team had much to be proud of.

The NHL instituted the shoot-out in 2005, and, every time a similar move is made, the player's described as "going Forsberg."

"It was and will always be a big part of my career," Forsberg said of the Lillehammer goal, "and something that catapulted me into celebrity status in the hockey world."

# Overtime Winner Sets Off Magical Playoff Run

# PAVEL BURE

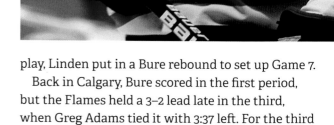

The Vancouver Canucks came within an inch of winning their first Stanley Cup championship in 1994, but the magical run was almost over before it began.

The Canucks boasted Pat Quinn as president, general manager and coach; captain Trevor Linden as leader on and off the ice; goalie Kirk McLean playing the best hockey of his life; and Pavel Bure, the most thrilling player in the game. But despite winning their division in 1992 and 1993, they capped each year with a loss in the second round of the playoffs. Entering the 1993–94 season, expectations in Vancouver were mountain high.

Their regular season, however, was mediocre, and Vancouver began the playoffs as the seventh seed in the Western Conference. Their first-round opponent was the Calgary Flames, who still had the core of their 1989 Stanley Cup–winning roster intact. The Canucks won Game 1, 5–0, but lost the next three, and Bure didn't score in any of the four games.

With the Canucks facing elimination in Game 5, Bure scored their only goal in regulation, and Geoff Courtnall added the overtime winner to extend the series. Game 6 also went to overtime, and on a power

play, Linden put in a Bure rebound to set up Game 7.

Back in Calgary, Bure scored in the first period, but the Flames held a 3–2 lead late in the third, when Greg Adams tied it with 3:37 left. For the third straight game, the teams were playing overtime.

Halfway through the first extra period, it looked as though the Flames finally had the goal they needed to clinch the series and end the Canucks' season. Bearing down on a 2-on-1, Theoren Fleury faked a shot and feathered a pass to Robert Reichel, who had a wide open net to shoot at. But McLean slid across and stopped the puck on the goal line. The goal judge and everyone watching thought it was in.

"I made the read, and when you do a two-pad slide, that's kind of a desperation move, but I timed it perfectly," recalled McLean 20 years later. "Theo threw a wonderful pass over to Reichel, and I was able to get my toe on it. Without a doubt, it was the most famous save of my career. It was a defining moment. And we all know what happened after that."

In the second overtime, Dave Babych dished the puck to Jeff Brown, who sent a tape-to-tape pass

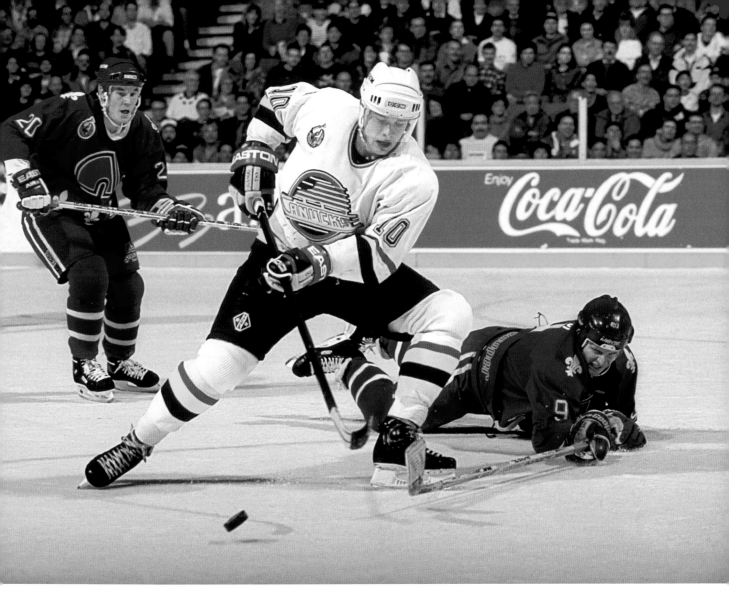

from blue line to blue line that Bure took at full speed. He was behind defenseman Zarley Zalapski in the blink of an eye, and with his deft touch on full display, he faked a backhand before putting the puck around Mike Vernon's outstretched pad at 2:20 to complete the comeback and win the series.

"As part of our practice routine, I had been going through quick counters from a defensive setup," said Quinn. "We probably practiced that every day. We had some real good passers — especially Jeff Brown — and part of making a good pass is that somebody had to get open. Pavel cut up through the middle, and that's where Brown hit him. As soon as that happened, our whole bench stood up because Pavel would make things happen when he had those sorts of opportunities. The rest was history."

The play was over in an instant, and Bure flung off his gloves as his teammates mobbed him. The stunned silence of the home crowd contrasted with the Canucks' wild celebration.

Vancouver carried that momentum all the way to Game 7 of the Stanley Cup Final.

After beating the Dallas Stars and Toronto Maple Leafs, the Canucks faced the Mark Messier–led New York Rangers in the championship series.

There, Vancouver faced another 3-1 series deficit but clawed its way back to tie the series. Down 3–2 late in Game 7 and carrying the play, the Canucks' Nathan Lafayette hit the post. Luck had run out for the team of destiny, and the Rangers ended a 54-year Stanley Cup drought with the win.

In 1994, Bure led the NHL in regular-season and playoff goals, and none was more memorable than his double-overtime winner in Game 7 against the Flames. At the time, Vancouver broadcaster Tom Larscheid called it the "greatest moment in Canucks history."

For a franchise that continues to seek its first championship, it still is.

# Rising Wrister Ends Longest Modern Game

# KEITH PRIMEAU

There had been longer games, but not since the Great Depression.

Keith Primeau's goal at 92:01 of overtime (in the *fifth* overtime period) in the early hours of May 5, 2000, ended what had become the third-longest game in NHL history. (In 1933, Ken Doraty scored for Toronto at 104:46 of overtime to defeat Boston, and a goal by Detroit's Mud Bruneteau beat the Montreal Maroons at 116:30 of extra time in 1936.)

Primeau was a 6-foot-5, 220-pound power forward who would end his career with 266 goals, 619 points and 1,541 minutes in penalties in 909 regular-season games, including three 30-goal seasons and seven years when he spent more than 100 minutes in the penalty box. But before he netted his tiebreaker in 2000, he had managed only 7 goals in 78 career play-off games.

The 1999–2000 season was Primeau's first year with the Philadelphia Flyers, and they finished at the top of the Eastern Conference. Facing cross-state rival Pittsburgh Penguins in the Eastern Conference semifinal, the Flyers lost the first two games at home. They got back into the series with an overtime win in Game 3 in Pittsburgh, which was where the teams met for Game 4 on May 4.

The Penguins opened the scoring in the first period, and the Flyers tied it on a power-play goal early in the third, their first in 17 chances in the series. The goal was reviewed to see if it might have gone in off a high stick, but it held up, and for a second straight game, the teams were playing overtime.

Just 30 seconds in, the Flyers' Daymond Langkow hit the post. Alexei Kovalev did the same for the Penguins early in the second extra frame, and in the third overtime, Pittsburgh had two power plays while Philadelphia had one, getting six shots, but neither team could score.

Four years earlier the Penguins had won a game with 45 seconds left in the fourth overtime, which had set a record for the longest game in modern NHL history. The teams blew past that into another 15-minute intermission.

"After a while guys were saying, 'What period is this?' 'The sixth — no, it's the eighth,'" said Penguins goalie Ron Tugnutt. "Your mind starts playing tricks on you."

Flyers coach Craig Ramsay was also suffering. "Into the last period, whatever it was, I didn't say a single thing," he said. "I just pointed to them when they came on the ice [to let them know] who would start. I was almost as exhausted as [they were]."

Primeau, however, was gaining strength: "As the game went on, I honestly started to feel better. There was a lot more room in the neutral zone, and I just wanted to try and capitalize."

And he did. Primeau picked up the puck at center ice and took it down the right side. When Penguins defenseman Darius Kasparaitis blocked his path, he cut back inside to the center of the right circle and fired a wrist shot. The 4,000 or so people still in the stands watched it rise over Tugnutt's shoulder and hit the back pipe of the net 12 minutes and 1 second into the fifth overtime.

With the Flyers' 72nd shot of the game, Primeau ended the game at 2:35 a.m., precisely seven hours after the opening faceoff.

"I didn't really see it so much as hear it," said Primeau after the game. "It was a great feeling. It didn't really sink in until everybody kind of dived on me.

"There were 20 heroes in that locker room. I was just the goal-scorer. Everybody's been on me to shoot more. I just tried to get the puck flat and get it on goal."

After losing an NHL-record eight straight overtime games in the playoffs, the Flyers had won two such games in a row to tie the series. And whether it was a momentum swing or losing the longest game in 64 years that broke the Penguins' collective back and spirit, the Flyers closed out the series in two more games.

While Primeau got the overtime winner, history wouldn't have been made without Flyers goalie Brian Boucher. Kovalev had scored at 2:22 of the first period, and then Boucher shut out the Penguins for the next 149:39 — leaving him just 21 seconds short of two and a half games' worth of shutout hockey.

There was a hero in the other room too. After being traded to Pittsburgh late in the 1999–2000 season, Tugnutt left in the off-season to sign with the Columbus Blue Jackets. His 70-save masterpiece that night was his NHL high point. He played four more seasons but never appeared in another playoff series.

## February 24, 2002

# Guiding Canada to Gold

# JOE SAKIC

Joe Sakic was a major factor in the two Stanley Cup championships the Colorado Avalanche won during his 20-year NHL career, and he helped lead Canadian national teams to gold medals in the World Cup, World Championship and World Junior Championship. Yet he never made more of a difference in a single game than he did during one glorious 60-minute stretch played in Salt Lake City, Utah.

On a team full of future Hall of Famers, "Burnaby Joe" was in on four of Team Canada's five goals — scoring the winning goal himself — as the Canadians beat the United States, 5–2, in the gold-medal game of the 2002 Winter Games. It was Canada's first Olympic men's hockey championship in 50 years.

"As a kid you dream of winning the Stanley Cup," Sakic said. "And as you get older, you understand the importance of winning the Olympics."

It was so important to Canadians that an estimated one-third of the entire population was glued to the television on the afternoon of February 24, the final day of the 2002 games, hoping to see Canada win its first men's Olympic championship since the Edmonton Mercurys took the title in 1952.

Steve Yzerman, Sakic's teammate on the legendary 2002 roster managed by Wayne Gretzky and coached by Pat Quinn, said the Americans and Canadians were relatively equal except for one thing: "We had Joe."

Throughout most of the Salt Lake Olympic tournament, Canada had been anything but dominant, losing its opener to Sweden, barely edging Germany and tying the Czech Republic in the opening round, and squeaking past Finland, 2–1, in the quarterfinals before hammering the surprising semifinalist, Belarus. That qualified them to meet the archrival Americans, who had slipped by Russia, 3–2, on the 22nd anniversary of the Miracle on Ice.

In Salt Lake City, as often happened in Colorado,

Sakic was asked to play with two of the team's less experienced wingers, Jarome Iginla and Simon Gagné, and the line soon became one of the best troikas in the tournament.

Unselfishness was already a hallmark of the Avalanche captain. Eight months earlier he had passed the Stanley Cup to Raymond Bourque without lifting it himself, so that the NHL veteran — then in his 22nd and final season and with his first Cup win — could be the first to hoist it.

In the final, Sakic set up Iginla, with 27 seconds left to go in the first period, to put Canada up 2–1. After Brian Rafalski tied the game fairly late in the second period, Sakic went to work again in the period's final minute, taking a pass in the slot and firing one of his trademark scorching wrist shots off U.S. defenseman Brian Leetch and past goalie Mike Richter, for the lead that Canada would never surrender.

The United States, playing on home ice, exerted heavy pressure in the third period but was held at bay by Martin Brodeur and some commendable Canadian defensive play.

With four minutes to go, Iginla gave Canada some breathing room, scoring on assists from Yzerman and Sakic, and in the game's next-to-last minute, Sakic scored the final goal, breaking in alone with an assist from Iginla. That set up a cross-country celebration and elevated the game into the same iconic stratosphere as Game 8 of the 1972 Summit Series. It also combined with the Canadian women's stirring victory of the previous day to give Canada a sweep over the United States at Salt Lake.

With 7 points, Sakic was chosen the tournament's most valuable player, and, apparently freed of the longtime Olympic jinx, Canada went on to win two of the next three Olympic gold medals.

"Having the chance to play for my country at the Olympics [he was also on the 1998 team and captained the 2006 squad] and especially winning a gold medal in Salt Lake City was an amazing and memorable experience I'll always cherish."

As will the rest of Canada.

## Dueling Hat Tricks

# SID THE KID VS. THE GREAT EIGHT

Drafted first overall one year apart, Alexander Ovechkin and Sidney Crosby couldn't have more disparate personalities, but they will be forever compared.

The Moscow-born Ovechkin, selected first by the Washington Capitals in 2004, is the brash extrovert. He's his generation's best sniper, a 6-foot-3, 239-pound juggernaut — an unstoppable force of personality and pure goal scoring.

Crosby, from Cole Harbour, Nova Scotia, was Pittsburgh's top pick in 2005. Off the ice he's more reserved, with the calm and maturity that came with bearing the mantle of the Next Big Thing, as Wayne Gretzky anointed him in his early teens. His game doesn't drop as many jaws, but the victories are starting to pile up.

Ovechkin's debut was delayed by the 2004–05 lockout, so the two entered the league together in 2005–06. In the post-Gretzky, post-lockout era, the NHL needed a crossover star to appeal to American audiences. It got two.

The two rookies didn't disappoint. Crosby, at 18, became the youngest player in NHL history to record 100 points, while 20-year-old Ovechkin won the Calder Trophy after becoming only the second rookie to register more than 50 goals and 100 points.

In 2006–07, Crosby had 120 points and won both the Art Ross and Hart Trophies. He was the youngest MVP in league history and the youngest scoring champion in the history of major professional sports.

In 2007–08, Ovechkin became the first player in 12 years to score 65 goals and won the first of two straight Hart Trophies.

To this point, any rivalry between the two was based more on a theoretical debate about who was the best player in the game. Although they both played in the Eastern Conference, their teams hadn't met in any significant way — until the 2009 playoffs.

That spring the second-seeded Capitals faced the fourth-seeded Penguins in the Eastern Conference semifinal, and Crosby opened the scoring in Game 1. Ovechkin scored later in the first period, and Washington went on to win, 3–2.

By Game 2 the bad blood was evident. There were nine penalties in a physical first period, with Crosby once again opening the scoring. Early in the second,

Alex Ovechkin (left) celebrates a goal on May 4, 2009. Sidney Crosby (right) scores one of his 3 goals on the same night.

Ovechkin responded, only to have Crosby get a 2nd goal eight minutes later. At the end of the second period, the score was tied at 2.

The third period was one for the history books. Ovechkin beat Marc-André Fleury with a one-timer on a power play, with 7:07 left, then blew a slap shot over Fleury's glove, with 4:38 remaining, for his 3rd goal of the game and 7th of the postseason.

Hats rained down from the Washington fans, and captain Crosby asked the referees to do something about it.

"People kept throwing hats, and I was just asking if he could make an announcement to ask them to stop," he said.

Crosby tried his best to end the party in the Washington stands. He completed his own hat trick on a power play in the final minute after Fleury was pulled for an extra attacker. It was his 8th goal of the playoffs, tops in the league.

Fans had witnessed one of the greatest 1-on-1 matchups the NHL has ever seen. Crosby may have had the last goal, but the Capitals won, 4–3, and took a 2-0 series lead. Ovechkin won this particular battle, but Crosby won the war. The Penguins took the next

three games and closed out the series in Game 7, with Crosby scoring twice in a 6–2 win. Crosby had 13 points in the series, but Ovechkin's 14 were the most in one series since 1995.

The Penguins went on to win the Stanley Cup, and Crosby became the youngest captain in league history to lift it.

While Ovechkin's career scoring numbers are higher, Crosby has had more team success, including two Olympic gold medals and another Stanley Cup, at the expense of Ovechkin's Capitals in Round 2, in 2016. But if they're keeping tabs on one another, neither is saying so.

"I never notice them acknowledging or comparing each other," says Capitals defenseman Matt Niskanen, who played with Crosby in Pittsburgh. "They both stay away from that. With that competitive nature, they have just a little bit of hate for each other, but I think at the same time they both respect each other's game. One probably wishes he had the other's skill set at times. I bet Sid wishes he had that kind of shot, that kind of threat from a distance that Ovie has, and I bet you Ovie sometimes wishes he had Sid's vision or his playmaking ability."

# Golden Goal

# SIDNEY CROSBY

C anada ended a 50-year gold-medal drought in men's hockey at the 2002 Winter Olympic Games in Salt Lake City, Utah, but followed that up with a dismal seventh-place finish in Turin, Italy, in 2006. With the 2010 Olympics being held in Vancouver, British Columbia, the national psyche would not survive another embarrassment on the ice.

These Olympics were already considered a litmus test of the country's self-image and of the way it was perceived around the world. Canada held the dubious distinction of being the only hosting country never to have won Olympic gold at home — at the Summer Games in Montreal, Quebec, in 1976 and again at the Winter Olympics in Calgary, Alberta, in 1988.

During the opening ceremony in Vancouver, the world was treated to the odd sight of Wayne Gretzky holding the Olympic torch, standing in the back of a pickup truck as he was driven through the rainy streets. Next up, an Olympic cauldron failed to deploy properly, as one of its arms malfunctioned.

But once the games began, Canadians settled in and enjoyed the party as the medals — gold included — rolled in in record numbers. But there was one medal that mattered most, and it was up to the men's hockey team to deliver it.

Scott Niedermayer was the captain, but Canada's hopes were pinned on the Next One from Cole Harbour, Nova Scotia.

Sidney Crosby had already won the Hart Trophy in just his second NHL season, 2006–07, and become the youngest captain in NHL history to win the Stanley Cup — with the Pittsburgh Penguins in 2009. He was the heir apparent to Canadian hockey royalty, and he carried the hopes and fears of a nation on his 22-year-old shoulders. He was also the embodiment of the way the country sees itself: humble, hard-working, tough and a winner.

Neither Crosby nor Team Canada inspired confidence early in the tournament. Crosby struggled to find chemistry with a series of wingers, and the team had a 1-1-1 record in the preliminary round, including a 5–3 loss to the United States.

The result of their mediocrity was a date with their old foes from Russia in the quarterfinals. With a stacked roster led by the Washington Capitals'

Sidney Crosby celebrates with teammates after scoring the golden goal (left) in 2010.

Alexander Ovechkin — the two-time reigning Hart Trophy winner — there was anxiety that Canada wouldn't reach the medal round.

But Canada was "like gorillas coming out of a cage," according to Russian goalie Ilya Bryzgalov, and got a monkey off its back by defeating Russia for the first time in nine tries at the Olympics. And the Canadians did it in dominant fashion, by a 7–3 score, using a combination of muscle and skill.

The semifinal was a white-knuckle affair, with Slovakia hitting the post in the dying moments of a 3–2 Canada win. That set up a gold-medal matchup with Team USA, held immediately before the closing ceremony. It was generally agreed that the nation's psyche would suffer grievous damage if its team lost — at its own game, on its own turf — to its big brother to the south.

The game was either going to provoke a national celebration or a national wake, and 80 percent of Canadian television viewers tuned in to find out.

Some 26.5 million Canadians watched some part of the game, a per-capita number that puts American Super Bowl ratings to shame.

Jonathan Toews, Canada's best player in the tournament, opened the scoring in the first period. The lead extended to 2–0 on a goal by Corey Perry in the second before Ryan Kesler got the Americans on the board.

It was still 2–1 late in the third period when the United States pulled goalie Ryan Miller, and with 24.4 seconds left, Zach Parise, whose father played for Team Canada in the 1972 Summit Series, pounced on a rebound and tied the game. The air was sucked out of the building, and the country's mood drooped.

Crosby had developed chemistry with Jarome Iginla in the elimination round, and in overtime of the gold-medal game, Crosby chipped the puck into the corner of the offensive zone. Iginla won a battle along the boards, and Crosby screamed for the puck as he circled towards the net. Iginla passed it as he was knocked to the ice, and the puck hardly touched Crosby's stick before he swept it between Miller's legs from the bottom of the left-hand faceoff circle, surprising the goalie and everyone else in the building.

At 7:40 of overtime, Canada had a 3–2 victory and the final gold medal of the Vancouver Olympics. It was the country's 14th, setting a new record for the most gold medals by one nation at a Winter Olympics.

Crosby flung his gloves and stick high in the air, and the enduring image is of Crosby's bare hands clenched, a look of pure joy on his face, as he waits for his teammates to catch up and mob him.

# Cup-Winning Goal Ends Chicago's Dry Spell

# PATRICK KANE

For a few excruciating moments, Chicago Blackhawks fans couldn't be sure their long wait was actually over.

But Patrick Kane knew right away.

It was the fifth minute of overtime in Game 6 of the 2010 Stanley Cup Final, and the multitalented Hawk winger, just 21 and appearing in the playoffs for only the second time in his career, had taken a feed from defenseman Bryan Campbell on the left side of the offensive zone, danced towards the Philadelphia Flyers net along the goal line and shot on goalie Michael Leighton's short side.

At that point, just about everyone in Philadelphia's Wachovia Center lost sight of the puck.

As Blackhawks radio play-by-play announcer John Wiedeman called it: "Loose puck in the crease … and … no! It's in the net. They score! They score! The Hawks win the Stanley Cup! The Hawks win the Stanley Cup! Leighton is down on his knees in the goal crease, and that one looked like it slid past him into the net. They're going to take a look upstairs."

But video review confirmed what Kane and teammate Patrick Sharp were already celebrating: the Hawks had broken the NHL's longest current Stan-ley Cup dry spell and won their first championship since 1961, when Bobby Hull and Stan Mikita were about Kane's age.

"Blackhawks fans around the world, you've endured 49 years of frustration, but your patience has finally paid off! Lord Stanley's new address is Sweet Home Chicago," Wiedeman enthused after officials had confirmed the puck was in the net.

The goal and the title that accompanied it were the final steps in a dramatic hockey turnaround in the Windy City. The Hawks had reached the Western Conference final the season before but had bowed out in five games to the Detroit Red Wings. Before that, Chicago had missed the playoffs for five straight seasons and in nine of the previous 10 years.

"It's a great moment, something that will stand out

Patrick Kane celebrates his Cup-winning goal, while officials (right) confirm the puck is in the net.

"I shot. I saw it go right through the legs, sticking right under the pad in the net," Kane said after the game. "I don't think anyone saw it in the net. I booked it to the other end. I knew it was in. I tried to sell the celebration a bit. It's pretty surreal."

Blackhawks head coach Joel Quenneville said the puck made a funny sound, "like hitting the back of the leather at the back of the net," and when officials lifted the net, "the puck fell through. So we knew that was the winner."

Kane's teammate John Madden had originally thrown his gloves into the corner when Kane started to celebrate, retrieved them when officials signaled that a video review was to take place, and then tossed them away for good when the goal was confirmed.

"It was pretty weird," Madden said. "It was like we won two Cups tonight."

When the Hawks went on to win the championship again in 2013 and 2015, reaching the conference final or better in five of seven seasons, the first mini-dynasty of the post-lockout era was born. Chicago's three Stanley Cups in six years equaled the total the Blackhawks franchise had managed over the first 84 years of its history.

Kane, Jonathan Toews, Marian Hossa, Duncan Keith, Brent Seabrook and Niklas Hjalmarsson were the core of the Hawks' triple Cup winners, in an era when the salary cap and strong Western Conference opposition made such an achievement unlikely.

in a lot of our careers for a long time — especially mine, with what happened," Kane said. "Nothing will ever take that moment and that day away."

The Flyers, who hadn't won the Cup in 35 years themselves, had forced overtime when Scott Hartnell tied the game at 3–3 with four minutes left in regulation time. Later, Jeff Carter just missed the net on a glorious chance, meaning Chicago was actually fortunate to get the extra period.

But Kane, who had scored 3 goals and added a pair of assists in the first five games of the final, solidified the new Windy City era with his shot, which lodged under the net's padding behind Leighton, shielded from the sight of everyone but Kane and Sharp. The goal light did not go on, and fans were surprised to see the Blackhawks celebrating.

# OT Winner Clinches Team's Fourth Straight Gold

# MARIE-PHILIP POULIN

Her teammates on the bench were hollering at her to shoot, but Laura Fortino made the choice that transported her, Marie-Philip Poulin and the 2014 Canadian women's team into Olympic hockey folklore.

Instead of firing towards the net, Fortino, an offensive defenseman who had spent the entire Olympic tournament concentrating mostly on defending against the fleet-footed American attack, passed the puck to her left to Poulin, the team's most timely sniper.

A moment later the puck went beyond goalie Jessie Vetter into the U.S. net to give Canada a 3–2 victory at 8:10 of overtime of the gold-medal showdown. Many Olympic observers say it's the greatest women's hockey game of all time.

"We needed shots, and I could hear them yelling to shoot," said Fortino, who, in her first Olympics, had 30 minutes and 21 seconds of ice time in the gold-medal game — the most of any player on either side. "I faked a shot, and I saw her wide open ... I had to give it to her."

It was the second goal of the match for Poulin, who had sent the game into overtime with just 54.6 seconds left in regulation time and Canadian goalie Shannon Szabados on the bench for an extra attacker. She had also scored both goals for Canada in the 2010 gold-medal victory over the United States.

"It's an amazing moment ... surreal," Poulin said right after her historic goal. "We all know it was a team effort. We never gave up. I'm so happy we got it back. It was a great journey."

It was Canada's fourth straight Olympic gold, after the United States won the inaugural championship at Nagano in 1998. Hayley Wickenheiser, Jayna Hefford and captain Caroline Ouellette all tied the Winter Olympic record — for any sport — with gold medals in four consecutive Olympics.

It was the most bitterly frustrating Olympic loss for the Americans, who had won four of the five previous world championships and four straight pre-Olympic games against Canada before the Canadians prevailed in the group stage of the tournament, also by a score of 3–2.

And Canada's head coach, Kevin Dineen, fired early in the season by the Florida Panthers, had been with

Marie-Philip Poulin (seen at right) scores the gold-medal-winning goal at the 2014 Sochi Olympics.

the team for barely two months after Dan Church resigned in mid-December.

In the final, the United States, playing a tactically perfect style, led 2–0 with less than four minutes to play in regulation time before Brianne Jenner scored on a deflection off an American defenseman with 3:26 left, and Poulin tied it from the side of the crease in the final minute.

Moments before the tying goal, Kelli Stack's shot from the American blue line curled to the left just before it could find the empty net and bounced off the post to keep Canadian hopes alive.

"That's how you just know it wasn't our night," said a devastated Stack. "The puck literally just missed going in by an inch."

Wickenheiser, the greatest female player in Canadian hockey history, who was playing what might have been her last Olympic game, used a curling reference to describe her thoughts on the near miss.

"I just said, 'Sweep, sweep it. Get it wide.' I didn't think it was going to go in by the angle, but you never know. It turned the game around, really gave

us another life. I mean, what a finish."

Canada again seemed doomed after being assessed a penalty in overtime with the teams already down to four skaters apiece, but almost immediately thereafter, the British referee gave the Americans a penalty. Canada was awarded a fourth skater instead of a penalty shot when Wickenheiser was hauled down on a breakaway.

On the ensuing power play, Fortino cradled the puck back and forth to inch an American forward out of position and then feathered the pass to Poulin for the golden goal.

"We did face a lot this year, and nobody will ever know the true adversity we faced unless you were part of it," Fortino said. "But I think that really helped us in this moment today. We came through when it counted.

"I don't think this moment will ever be comparable to anything."

# INDEX